# THE

# FOUR

# MISTAKES

# THE

# FOUR

# MISTAKES

## AVOIDING THE
## LEGAL LANDMINES
## THAT LEAD TO
## BUSINESS DISASTER

MICHAEL G. TRACHTMAN, ESQ.

STERLING

New York / London
www.sterlingpublishing.com

STERLING and the distinctive Sterling logo are registered trademarks
of Sterling Publishing Co., Inc.

**Library of Congress Cataloging-in-Publication Data**
Trachtman, Michael G.
The four mistakes : avoiding the legal landmines that lead to business disaster / Michael
G. Trachtman.
   p. cm.
ISBN 978-1-4027-6817-0
1. Business law--United States. 2. Business enterprises--Law and legislation--United
States--Popular works. I. Title.
KF889.85.T73 2010
346.7307--dc22

2009040773

2  4  6  8  10  9  7  5  3  1

Published by Sterling Publishing Co., Inc.
387 Park Avenue South, New York, NY 10016
© 2010 by Michael G. Trachtman

Distributed in Canada by Sterling Publishing
*c/o* Canadian Manda Group, 165 Dufferin Street
Toronto, Ontario, Canada M6K 3H6
Distributed in the United Kingdom by GMC Distribution Services
Castle Place, 166 High Street, Lewes, East Sussex, England BN7 1XU
Distributed in Australia by Capricorn Link (Australia) Pty. Ltd.
P.O. Box 704, Windsor, NSW 2756, Australia

Sterling ISBN 978-1-4027-6817-0

For information about custom editions, special sales, premium and
corporate purchases, please contact Sterling Special Sales
Department at 800-805-5489 or specialsales@sterlingpublishing.com.

To Jen. She knows why.

# CONTENTS

## AUTHOR'S NOTE

A brief word about style . . . After consulting a variety of style manuals, and after struggling with the use of "he or she," "him or her," and other ways to achieve gender neutrality, I opted for the simplistic and traditional use of "he," "his," and "him" when referring to no one in particular—as in, "The ADA defines a 'qualified' employee as one who can perform the 'essential functions' of his job," or "A nondisclosure/nonuse agreement with these provisions can prevent him from taking important data to a competitor." I did this purely to minimize textual awkwardness, and I hope that nothing other than a preference for simpler sentences will be read into my stylistic choices.

# THE

# FOUR

# MISTAKES

# "I Was Doing Great.
# How Could This Happen?"

THIS BOOK IS FOR BUSINESS OWNERS, EXECUTIVES, AND MANAGERS who want to protect their companies, their careers, and their futures from one of the most insidious and misunderstood risks there is—the law.

Your competition's unmanaged risks are your opportunities, and this book will provide substantial advantages for business owners, executives, and managers seeking a competitive edge. Much of the information and strategies detailed in the following chapters can be utilized not only as a shield, but also as a sword.

Business is, in substantial part, the art of foreseeing and managing risk. To most businesspeople, however, the risks posed by our laws and legal system are largely unknown and seemingly unknowable. The upshot is that, much too frequently, these kinds of risks remain back-burnered and unresolved, until it's too late and a costly and embarrassing lawsuit or legal setback hits the fan. Then—after the attorneys' fees, the wasted time, the insurance complications, the upset and distraction, the financial losses, the lost opportunities, the adverse publicity—the ugly, frustrating truth emerges: had those in charge known just a bit more about the law's mysterious (and sometimes arbitrary) requirements, all the tribulations could have been easily avoided.

For more than thirty years, I've spent my professional life getting businesses out of legal trouble and training the people who run them in the art of staying out of legal trouble. Here's what I've learned: although, as the maxim goes, ignorance of the law is no excuse, maybe it *should* be. I hear the same thing all the time. "The law says *what*? That makes no sense. How was I supposed to know about *that*?" Business owners, executives, and managers feel trapped in a world where, almost inevitably, they or someone who works for them will unwittingly run afoul of the law, for which an unholy price will be paid. In so many crucial aspects, business has become a game governed by a rule book the players can't understand.

This fact of business life can have disastrous consequences. The popular media routinely report on the seemingly fit and healthy athlete or celebrity who suffers a premature death because of a lurking, undetected condition. "If only he had undergone a simple test and taken the appropriate medication," the television doctors tell us, "this never would have happened." Thanks to the law's traps and pitfalls, the same thing happens, all too often, to seemingly fit and healthy businesses. Many of them function with camouflaged legal risk factors that, when triggered, cause unforeseen and overwhelming, yet fully avoidable, losses.

I've seen too many businesses and businesspeople get blindsided. I've seen enough of the hardships unmanaged legal risks can inflict. This book represents my effort to practice preventive legal medicine.

There is, of course, no one-size-fits-all fix, but there are clearly discernible links between certain actions and inactions and certain results, and these links teach us the fundamental axioms that apply to virtually all businesses. To continue the medical analogy, through experience and study, doctors now know the links between, for example, certain lifestyle choices and heart disease and cancer. From these links, the fundamental axioms of a healthier, more preventive lifestyle can be gleaned. The same is true in business. Lawyers who spend their careers getting businesses out of trouble learn what gets them into trouble. Lawyers who train executives and managers to stay out of trouble learn which business solutions work on paper and which work in the real world. Patterns and associations surface.

This book is about the prime offenders, what I call the Four Mistakes—the law-related actions and oversights that cause the most damage most frequently and that point the way toward business solutions that make the law an ally, not an enemy. These Four Mistakes hold a convenient truth: many successful businesses suffer the same problems for the same reasons and can utilize the same preventive measures to keep history from repeating itself.

Owners and operators of small and medium-sized businesses will recognize the Four Mistakes as involving the issues and worries they confront on a daily basis and, often, in the middle of the night. So will executives and managers who work in larger or publicly held companies—those responsible for top-level management, as well as those responsible for individual departments or teams within the larger organization, are burdened by these same problems. The Four Mistakes are, unfortunately, universal and scalable.

You can't avoid a risk unless you know it's there. The first purpose of this book is to provide business executives and managers the knowledge that is power—the knowledge to understand and then evade a widely misapprehended battery of potentially devastating business risks that can, before you know it, turn your successes into failures.

The other side to that coin is this: Business executives and managers who do understand the Four Mistakes will learn how to take advantage of those who don't. For instance, you'll learn that one of the Four Mistakes involves the failure to effectively secure top employees from the reach of competitors. Having learned how to avoid making this mistake, you'll be equipped to recognize and capitalize on your competition's failure to implement the required safeguards—you'll be able to add to your talent pool while depleting theirs. The same is true with respect to many of the other topics that follow, such as boxing your adversaries in through e-mail documentation techniques, and learning how to include subtle deal terms that will give you the ability to negotiate from strength if things go awry. The Four Mistakes are, in this sense, the four opportunities.

Ultimately, I offer this book as a resource for those who wish to learn from the mistakes of others instead of their own.

# CHAPTER ONE

# The First Mistake: Losing the Documentation War

MOST SUCCESSFUL BUSINESS OWNERS, executives, and managers focus on doing the right thing. They know that over the long term reputation matters, and they understand that what goes around comes around. They're fair with their customers, they treat their employees well, and they deal honorably with their suppliers, consultants, and investors. Their expectation is that by playing it straight, others will reciprocate, and distracting and expensive disagreements and disharmony will be minimized.

But, unfortunately, doing the right thing is not always enough—disputes inevitably arise, the legal system takes over, and, at that point, doing the right thing is not nearly as important as being able to *prove* you did the right thing. As Justice Oliver Wendell Holmes Jr. is reputed to have once lectured a lawyer, "This is a court of *law*, young man, not a court of justice." There's a difference. You can be deemed a liar even though you were totally honest, and you can be ruled to have broken the law even though you scrupulously complied with it. In our legal system, it is proof, not reality, that is truth, and the failure to understand and plan for this bedrock precept leads many businesses to suffer a heavy, sometimes life-threatening price. There's only one way out of this conundrum: you *must* win the documentation war.

> ⤏ In our legal system, it is proof, not reality, that is truth, and the failure to understand and plan for this bedrock precept leads many businesses to suffer a heavy, sometimes life-threatening price.

# Understanding the Problem:
## The "My Word Against Your Word" Issue

The primary battleground on which the documentation war is fought involves business disputes in which one side accuses the other of saying or doing or intending something that the other side denies having said or done or intended. These omnipresent and frustrating "my word against your word" clashes are virtually inevitable, and they often evolve into dangerous and debilitating lawsuits. They spring from many sources. Sometimes, people honestly recollect facts in different ways. Sometimes, they interpret statements and events differently. Sometimes, their recollections are skewed over time by their self-interest. Sometimes, they out right lie to protect their job and bank account. But no matter the cause, every day in courtrooms across the country, the truth becomes an unfortunate casualty in these battles, and disconsolate litigants learn, the hard way, that there are few things more frustrating and expensive than knowing you're right and not being able to prove it.

Documents minimize the business and personal ruin these "my word against your word" disputes inflict. Documents can nip phony claims in the bud, they can expose lies and create credibility, and they can tilt the balance of power in favor of whoever has them. When faced with a choice between an uncorroborated memory and a reliable document, judges and juries will choose the document almost every time. Most businesspeople and, just as important, their lawyers understand that fact of life. As a result, once you show an adversary that you can document your position much

⋯⇢ **Documents minimize the business and personal ruin these "my word against your word" disputes inflict. Documents can nip phony claims in the bud, they can expose lies and create credibility, and they can tilt the balance of power in favor of whoever has them. When faced with a choice between an uncorroborated memory and a reliable document, judges and juries will choose the document almost every time.**

more effectively than he can, the door to a quick and favorable settlement opens. No rational businessperson wants to fight a fight he knows he'll probably lose.

A "my word against your word" battle can be a make or break point for a company or a career, and whichever side wins the documentation war will usually come out on top. Documents are the difference makers.

---

### The Case of Goode Manufacturing vs. Moore Company

"Call your next witness, Ms. Fairley."

"Your Honor, the plaintiff calls Mr. Moore."

Owen Moore felt the eyes of each juror as he walked toward the witness chair. He had founded and then run Moore Company for more than twenty years and was used to always being in control, always setting the direction of the discourse, always being on top of the variables. Not now. He knew that this was different, foreign, uncontrollable. Louis D. Case, his longtime lawyer and friend, had stressed that deference, almost to the point of subservience, was now the key: "Susan Fairley knows what she's doing. She's going to cross-examine you hard, and it's not going to be easy. Just listen to the question, and answer the question. Don't fence with her. It will make you look shifty, like you're trying to hide something." Moore was accustomed to assessing for himself if a question was worth answering or if it was time to move on to another subject. Part of him felt like a student who had been summoned to the principal's office. Part of him felt like an accused criminal in a police interrogation room.

The events that brought Moore to the courtroom began about a year before when Lucas Goode, the owner of Goode Manufacturing, came to see Moore in his office. Moore had a very clear recollection of the conversation. Goode was a longtime customer, and he told Moore that he was prepared to place a major order so long as Moore could provide a substantial discount and an installment-payment arrangement that would shift most of the payments to the next fiscal year. Moore agreed.

Goode also said he preferred delivery in six weeks. Moore told Goode that the usual delivery time was twelve weeks, but he would do what he could, no guarantees. They shook hands on the deal, and because of their longstanding relationship, Moore dispensed with the usual paperwork.

Six weeks later, Goode called, asking why the order had not been delivered.

"It's in process. I accelerated it. It'll be there in another two weeks at most," Moore told him.

"What! You promised me delivery by *now*." Goode was panicked. "I told you we had to have it in six weeks. We're going to lose 3 million dollars in pure profit unless you can produce."

"I *told* you no guarantees," said Moore. "I never would have made the deal if I knew you had to have it in six weeks."

"You're reinventing history, Owen. This is out of my hands. Our company is not going to eat this loss. You are."

Three days later, Moore was served with a lawsuit alleging that Moore had breached the delivery agreement. The lawsuit sought $3 million in compensatory damages as well as punitive damages for fraud and named the Moore Company and Moore individually as defendants. After the usual (and expensive) procedural wrangling and pretrial discovery inquiries, Moore and Goode met face to face, along with their counsel, to see if a compromise could be worked out.

"You know you blew this, Lucas. You know I never guaranteed a six-week delivery date. I'm sorry if this got you into trouble, but you can't blame this on me."

"I know no such thing, Owen. I want the 3 million dollars and not a penny less. It's my word against your word, and I'm betting the jury will believe me. At this point, I've got no downside and may as well give it a go. If you're willing to roll the dice, so am I."

Moore was seething. He called his attorney later that night. "I did nothing wrong, Lou. You know the ropes. I'm out of my element. Can't you do anything?"

"Sure. I can punch and counterpunch with the best of them. But I've got to be honest with you, Owen. Susan Fairley is an excellent lawyer, and you haven't given me much to work with."

Moore took in the view from the witness stand and tried to steady himself. The judge sat to Moore's right, elevated on the bench, austere, literally above it all. The twelve jurors were stationed to his left. They looked at him skeptically, most likely recalling the opening statement delivered by Goode's lawyer, Susan Fairley, two days earlier. Fairley told the jurors, with great flourish, that she would prove to them that Moore was an unethical businessman who would say and do anything if there was money to be made. Fairley now sat at plaintiff's counsel table behind her customary array of color-coded three-ring binders. During the previous two days of trial, Moore had seen Fairley quickly extract from those binders any fact or document she needed at any time.

"You may proceed, Ms. Fairley."

Fairley walked from counsel table to a podium, about fifteen feet in front of the witness stand where Moore sat. "Please state your name and occupation for the record."

"Owen Moore. I am the CEO of Moore Company."

"Your Honor, plaintiff, Goode Manufacturing, calls Mr. Moore as on cross-examination."

Case had warned Moore that the trial might unfold in this way. "Goode Manufacturing is the plaintiff and they get to go first," Case told him. "Fairley will put Goode, her client, on the stand to give his version of the facts. She'll call a variety of other witnesses as well. She also has the right to call *you* as a witness. It's termed 'calling a witness as on cross-examination,' and it gives her the right to take a shot at you before I get to put you on the stand. She won't give you much of an opportunity to say what you want to say, believe me. She'll be trying to make you look bad on her terms before we get our chance to present our side of the story."

Fairley had put Goode on the stand earlier that morning. It was all Moore could do to control himself as he sat next to Case at counsel table. Goode was handsome, smooth, a great storyteller in the con-man genre— he knew when to make eye contact, he knew how to make himself look sympathetic, and he was unavoidably likable. Fairley took him through the chronology and eventually got to the six-week delivery issue.

"Mr. Goode, did you and Mr. Moore ever discuss a delivery date?"

"Yes, we certainly did."

"Was the delivery date important to you?"

"It was crucial."

"Why was that?"

"We needed the Moore components to complete the assembly of a complex system we were building for our best customer. We were under a strict deadline—our contract with our customer provided that if we did not deliver on time, we would forgo 3 million dollars in profit. Unless we got the Moore components in six weeks, we would not be able to meet our deadline. The delivery date was the key to the whole deal."

"Did you explain that to Mr. Moore?"

"Yes, in no uncertain terms. I told him that if he could not meet the deadline, I would understand, and it would not affect our future business relationship. I would get the product from another supplier. If he could meet the deadline, great. We had a long relationship, and I wanted to stick with him if I could because I knew him. But if he said he could meet the deadline, I told him he had to be absolutely positive, no excuses, not one day's delay, or we would lose 3 million dollars we could not afford to lose. If he had any insecurity about meeting the deadline, he *had* to tell me."

"What did Mr. Moore say in response to that?"

"He said it was no problem, and that he might even be able to deliver in five weeks. I again asked if he was sure. He said he understood the situation, and we could count on him."

"Did you believe him?"

"I did. We had a good relationship for many years. We never had a problem. I trusted him."

"What's the next thing that happened?"

"We shook hands on it, and Mr. Moore told me not to worry."

"Mr. Goode, did you take any notes respecting what happened at the meeting?"

"I did. I took notes as we talked. I'm a note taker. I always take notes when I am in an important meeting."

Fairley walked to the blue binder, deftly clicked it open, turned to a green-tabbed page, removed two documents, and walked back to the podium. The jury attentively watched the show.

"Mr. Goode, I show you a document marked Plaintiff's Exhibit 34. Can you identify it?"

"Yes. It's the original of my notes."

"Please read to the jury the highlighted portion of Plaintiff's Exhibit 34."

"'Told Moore about the six-week deadline. Told him it was mandatory. He said it was no problem, and we might have product in five weeks. Told him that we would lose 3 million dollars if he did not deliver on time. He said no problem.'"

"Do your notes accurately state what happened during your meeting with Mr. Moore?"

"Yes, absolutely."

"Mr. Goode, I now show you a document marked Plaintiff's Exhibit 35. Can you identify it?"

"Yes, it is a memo I dictated to our file from my notes. I sent the memo to my shareholders as soon as I got back to my office."

"Please read the highlighted portion to the jury."

"'I met with Owen Moore to see if Moore Company could meet the six-week delivery requirement. Moore assured me that it was no problem and told me he might be able to deliver in five weeks. I stressed to him that we would lose 3 million dollars if he blew the deadline, and he again told me it would be no problem. We then finalized the deal.'"

"Does your memo accurately state what happened during your meeting with Mr. Moore?"

"Yes. My memo is absolutely accurate."

"Why did you write this memo?"

"It's part of my job. On something this big and important, I had to report to my shareholders in writing, and I had to make sure my actions were confirmed in the files in case anything happened to me. This is part of our company's standard practice."

"No further questions, Your Honor."

Case cross-examined Goode as best as he could. Case implied that Goode could have created the notes and the memo long after the fact, to cover up his own mistake in not getting a real commitment from Moore.

"I suppose I could have made it all up, but I didn't, Mr. Case," Goode calmly explained. "I took an oath to God to tell the truth, and that's what I've done." A statement like that from most witnesses would have come off as trying too hard. But Goode made it work and then brought it down to business realities. "You need to understand something else, Mr. Case. We have standard, written documentation procedures in our company. This was nothing unusual. I keep notes and do memos like this all the time, every day, as a matter of course. You've seen my files. You know I've got reams of notes and memos. This is how we do business."

Case asked why Goode had not sent a confirming e-mail to Moore. Case intimated that if there really had been a crucial delivery deadline, Goode, an experienced businessman, would have confirmed it to Moore in writing to be certain that there would be no misunderstanding. But Fairley had prepared her witness very well.

"In hindsight, I wish I had sent him an e-mail, but that's not the way Owen and I typically did business. We've dealt with each other for many years, and we trusted each other. He would have been insulted if he got an e-mail like that from me. He knew I would have been insulted if he said he needed paperwork to back up my word—that's why he didn't ask me to submit a purchase order, and he didn't hit me with any of the usual Moore

Company sales forms. We have always done business on a handshake, and that's what we did in this instance."

Case had nowhere left to go—continuing to argue with Goode would not help and would likely alienate the jury. Case knew his only hope was Moore's ability to convince the jury that Moore was right and Goode was either lying or mistaken. Case spoke to Moore shortly before he took the stand.

"We're in a 'my word against your word' battle, Owen. *I* know you're telling the truth, and *you* know you're telling the truth, but that's not enough. You need to convince *the jury* that you're telling the truth."

"And just how do I do that? Goode had them eating out of his hand."

"Jurors don't have a truth-o-meter, Owen. They have no way to tell who is telling the truth. Good liars win cases all the time. Jurors go with their gut impressions."

"Great. So what do I do?"

"Look the jurors in the eye. Make human contact with them," Case counseled. "You have to be respectful but confident. Assertive, but not overly so. You know what someone looks like when he's being truthful. Make them believe you. You can do it."

"I'm not an actor, Lou. I'm a CEO."

Fairley arranged her notes on the podium. Several jurors leaned forward.

"Mr. Moore, do you have a perfect memory?"

Moore knew it was not quite a "When did you stop beating your wife?" question, but it was close. If he said he had a perfect memory, Fairley would ask him all sorts of questions about past events that Moore could not possibly remember, and make him look like the liar Fairley said Moore was in her opening statement. If Moore said he did not have a perfect memory . . . Moore was trapped, and he knew it.

"No. I have a very good memory, but of course, it's not perfect."

"Do you work hard, Mr. Moore?"

"I do."

"Do you sometimes work nights and weekends?"

"Yes."

"And that's because you have a lot of responsibilities and a lot of things to accomplish, right?"

"Yes, that's true."

"Do you have frequent meetings, telephone calls, that sort of thing?"

"I do."

"Do you have lots of things you have to keep track of and remember?"

"Yes, I suppose that's fair."

Moore kept reminding himself of Case's advice: don't fence with her; just answer the questions.

"Do you keep a written to-do list at work, Mr. Moore?"

"I do."

"And that's because, in view of all you have to do, you can't possibly keep it all in your head. Isn't that right, Mr. Moore?"

"Yes, I keep a to-do list so I won't lose track of or forget the things I have to get done."

"And that's because, as you've admitted, you don't have a perfect memory. Correct?"

"I don't have a perfect memory, but as I said I have a very good one."

"Do you submit a weekly expense report for reimbursement to the company, Mr. Moore?"

"I do."

"And do you keep a written record of the expenses as they are incurred?"

"I do."

"And that's because, with all you have to do, and given that you don't have a perfect memory, you couldn't possibly remember all your expenses unless you wrote them down, right?"

"I suppose."

"Do you periodically review Moore Company's financial statements?"

"I do."

"And do you focus on such key elements as gross receipts, general and administrative expenses, costs of sales, professional expenses, that sort of thing?"

"Yes, among other items."

"Can you remember those numbers off the top of your head, as you sit here?"

"Not all of them."

"And it's true, isn't it, that when you need accurate financial numbers you refer back to the written financial statements, which you keep handy in your office, right?"

"Yes."

"And again, that's because you don't have a perfect memory, right?"

"I already told you that, Ms. Fairley."

"No need to be defensive, Mr. Moore. Nothing to be ashamed of. I don't have a perfect memory either—that's why I have my notes in front of me with the points I want to cover with you. That's why I keep my documents in notebooks. OK?"

"OK."

"Now, you admit, don't you, that you had a meeting about a year and a half ago with Mr. Goode. Isn't that right?"

"Yes, we had a meeting."

"And in that meeting, the subject of a six-week delivery date was raised by Mr. Goode, correct?"

"Yes, the subject was raised."

"Now, it's your position that in that meeting, even though the subject of a six-week delivery date was raised, you never guaranteed delivery in six weeks, is that right?"

"That is correct. I never did."

"And you understand that Mr. Goode has a different recollection than you do about what you did or did not guarantee in terms of a delivery date. Right?"

"I heard him testify. He's wrong."

"Now, Mr. Moore, would you be so kind as to show the jury the notes you took at that meeting?"

"I didn't take any notes."

"OK. Then would you be so kind as to show the jurors the file memo you created after the meeting so you'd have a record of what was discussed?"

"I created no file memo."

"I see. Would you show the jury whatever documents you referred to for the purpose of accurately recalling what happened at that meeting that took place a year and a half ago?"

"I did not refer to any documents."

"Well, then, what did you rely on for purposes of making sure your recollection of what was said at that meeting is completely accurate?"

"I relied on my memory."

Fairley faced the jury, smirking. "That would be the *imperfect* memory we discussed earlier, correct?"

"You've made your point, Ms. Fairley."

"Sorry, Mr. Moore. We're not done yet. Do you remember creating *any* documents right after your meeting with Mr. Goode that confirmed what *really* happened at the meeting?"

"I do not recall any such documents, Ms. Fairley."

"Well, let's see if we can do something about that memory of yours, Mr. Moore." She walked from the podium back to the notebooks. Moore struggled to hide his unease. Fairley ceremoniously clicked open the red binder, removed a document, and clicked it shut. The clicks had become a signal to the jury to pay attention, that something dramatic was coming. The jurors watched Fairley closely as she moved from the podium to the notebooks and back to the podium.

"I show you a document that has been marked as Plaintiff's Exhibit 77. Can you identify it?"

"It's an e-mail I sent to my production manager."

"You sent this right after your meeting with Mr. Goode, correct?"

"That's right."

"Please read the highlighted portion to the jury, Mr. Moore."

"'This is an important order for one of our best customers. They say they've got to have the components in six weeks. Put everything else that doesn't have a deadline attached to it aside, and make it happen.'"

"So, Mr. Moore, does this help you remember that, *in fact*, Mr. Goode told you, *as you say in your own e-mail*, that he *had* to have these components within six weeks? Not that it would be nice to have them in six weeks. Not that he would be happy if he had them in six weeks. But that he *had* to have them in six weeks?"

"Mr. Goode told me that he wanted the components in six weeks, not that he absolutely had to have them in six weeks."

"So you lied to your own production manager?"

"No, Ms. Fairley. I wanted to motivate him. I told Mr. Goode we would do our best to get the components to him in six weeks, and that's what I was doing in this e-mail."

Fairley left the podium, walked toward the witness stand, and positioned herself uncomfortably close to Moore, within two or three feet of him.

"Come now, Mr. Moore. You didn't tell your production manager to do his best. You told him to drop everything and make it happen—*period*." Fairley raised her voice, angry and indignant. "You gave him the kind of order, the kind of unconditional command a CEO gives when he *knows* he's made a *commitment* that *must* be honored, didn't you, Mr. Moore?"

"It was a figure of speech, Ms. Fairley."

"Tell me, Mr. Moore, was your memory of the meeting better a year and a half ago, when the meeting took place? Or is it better now, a year and a half later, *after* you've been sued and you're worried about how you're going to pay the millions of dollars in damages you caused my client to suffer?"

Case bolted from his chair. "Objection, Your Honor. Ms. Fairley is . . ."

The judge interrupted. "Sustained. Back off, Ms. Fairley."

"Sorry, Your Honor. These kinds of things upset me, and I apologize. I'll withdraw the question." Fairley walked back to counsel table, her back toward Moore and the judge so they could not see her face. She smiled at the jurors. "Mr. Moore's right. I've made my point. No further questions." Several of the jurors smiled back. Several others glared at Moore.

Moore and Case went to dinner that night. "Owen, we need to be realistic. I don't think the jury bought into your testimony as much as they bought into Goode's. Goode has his notes and the memo. In order to find in our favor, the jury would have to believe that he committed a total fraud and fabricated the documents. I don't think that's likely."

"I understand that."

"Fairley boxed you in. We know what you meant by the e-mail, but she planted a seed. It doesn't matter what's true anymore. It's all about appearances. They've got documents. We don't. Juries love documents."

"I get it."

"Owen, I know this hurts. But we need to settle this case for whatever discount we can get, before it gets worse."

Moore thought for a moment, trying to tamp down his anger and frustration so he could realistically assess what he faced. "This isn't right, Lou."

"I know. But there's often a big difference between who's right and who wins."

"That's how the system works? They kidnap the truth and all I can do is pay the ransom?" Moore stopped short. "I apologize. I know this isn't your fault. I know you can only play the cards you're dealt."

Moore sat back, finally resigned to the maddening fact that he had run out of alternatives. "Make this go away, Lou. Now."

■ ■ ■

# Creating the Solution:
# E-Mail and Other
# Weapons of Mass Destruction

The message of the fictional (but, in a larger sense, true) case of *Goode Manufacturing vs. Moore Company*, and the countless real world cases like it, is worth repeating: *right does not make might*. You can be right and be found by a court to have been wrong. It is ammunition, not necessarily rectitude, that matters the most in litigation, and in the ubiquitous "my word against your word" world, documents are the weapons of mass destruction.

⇢ **Chances are that your e-mails are already creating ample documentation—sometimes in your favor, sometimes not. E-mail has changed the documentation universe, and before anything else, you'll need to understand and manage the perils of unintentional documentation.**

To avoid being victimized by this fact of business life, and to instead be able to profit from it, you need to learn how to harness the power of documents for your advantage. There are three facets to this process:

First, like Owen Moore, chances are that your e-mails are already creating ample documentation—sometimes in your favor, sometimes not. E-mail has changed the documentation universe, and before anything else, you'll need to understand and manage the perils of unintentional documentation.

Second, you can't document everything. You'll need to pick your shots. To do that, you'll need to develop a way to tell the difference between what you can let pass and what you better nail down.

Third, once you've decided that something needs documenting, you'll need to decide exactly how to do it. That requires a working knowledge of the documentation arsenal and how best to use what's in it.

## Step One: The Perils of Unintentional Documentation

In the spring of 2007, two senior hedge-fund managers at Bear Stearns exchanged a series of e-mails about the declining financial health of their funds. "We're in bad shape," one wrote to the other. But despite what they knew, they told investors the funds were fine. One even e-mailed the other, bragging about how successful he had been in hiding the truth about the funds. "Believe it or not— I've been able to convince people to add more money." The funds collapsed, and about a year later, the fraud indictments hit. The headline in *The New York Times*: "Prosecutors Build Bear Stearns Case on E-Mails."

In the *United States vs. Microsoft* antitrust proceeding, a key contention was that Microsoft was conspiring against Sun Microsystems. An internal Bill Gates e-mail surfaced in which he asked, "Do we have a clear plan on what we want Apple to do to undermine Sun?" A Microsoft executive e-mailed Gates with a strategy to force Apple to do Microsoft's bidding by threatening that, otherwise, Microsoft "will do a great deal of harm to Apple immediately." The damning e-mails became an embarrassing centerpiece in the case.

Monica Goodling, former counsel to then–U.S. Attorney General Alberto Gonzales, sent an e-mail to another official, directing him to draw up a policy giving her unprecedented (and unlawful) authority to hire and fire staffers based on politics and ideology, not competence. With seeming knowledge of the nature of what she was doing, she e-mailed the official, "send directly up to me, outside of the system." In another e-mail, she directed Department of Justice personnel to destroy documents, even though a congressional investigation was ongoing.

In June 2002, the Arthur Andersen accounting firm was convicted of obstructing the Securities and Exchange Commission's investigation into the collapse of Enron. Among the most damning pieces of evidence: an e-mail by Andersen's in-house counsel instructing an Andersen partner to remove incriminating language from an internal Andersen memo.

E-mails exposed that Merrill Lynch analysts were, among themselves, condemning stocks as "disasters" or "dogs," while they publicly promoted them to investors. Enron executives sent copious, incriminatory e-mails referring to meetings that they later claimed they never had, discussing plans to exercise political influence, and ruminating on how to derail pending and expected investigations. Authorities learned through e-mails that Credit Suisse First Boston staff was ordered to "clean up" files, leading to obstruction of justice charges.

And so on . . .

There is a strange, psychological aspect to e-mail. We seem to be willing to say in an e-mail what we'd never say in a memo or a letter. It is as if we think hard-copy documents could easily be discovered and used against us and, therefore, must be worded with great care, while e-mails have only an ephemeral and private existence and, therefore, can be dashed off quickly and without worry.

Of course, the opposite is true. Aside from the fact that e-mails are frequently printed and stored in the same paper files that hold memos and correspondence, they have an electronic life that is extremely difficult to extinguish. E-mails can be forwarded to a geometrically expanding array of unknown destinations with only a keystroke, and copies can remain on untold numbers of individual hard drives. E-mails can also remain on the servers through which they pass and the backup systems that routinely create copies of them. An entire industry devoted to the arcane art of finding, recovering, and analyzing the content of e-mails has arisen—and the inability to locate and resurrect a forgotten or even deleted e-mail is quickly becoming the exception and not the rule.

Here's the point: when you are writing an e-mail, you *must* take into consideration that, someday, it could easily become Exhibit A in a courtroom, blown up on a screen for all to read and criticize, and fair game for the media, your competition, and anyone else who has any use for it. "But that was a private e-mail," I frequently hear. Sorry. With limited exceptions (for instance, certain attorney-client communications), *there is no such thing as a private e-mail*, any more than there are private memos, letters, handwritten notes, or anything else. Virtually everything, no matter how personal, embarrassing, unintended, or incriminating, is subject to discovery and public display.

This reality has made e-mail sleuthing a key focus for the lawyers involved in business disputes, and with alarming frequency, these efforts pay large dividends. Picture a lawsuit in which one company claims that another owes it several million dollars. Then an e-mail exchange between executives surfaces. "I know we owe them the money, but if we keep denying it and running up their legal fees, they'll probably have to fold." Picture a lawsuit in which one company charges that there are defects in a product it bought from another company. An e-mail between middle managers is uncovered. "This thing doesn't work the way it should, but the directive from the top is to cover it up until we can make the changes." These kinds of smoking-gun e-mails pop up often enough to make the costs involved in e-mail retrieval and analysis well worth the investment.

···⟩ **E-mails must be written with the knowledge that they are not private and that they can live forever. If it will damage you, don't write it. If it will embarrass you, don't write it. Every time your fingers move to the keyboard, give yourself a private Miranda warning: everything you say can and will be held against you.**

Remember: it's not only the "smoking-gun" e-mails that will turn the tide. Those kinds of e-mails are relatively rare—more often, it's an e-mail like the one Owen Moore sent to his production manager that will be parsed and thrown back into your face. In the right context, sloppy phraseology can be a killer. Had Moore been thinking, he would have realized that with every e-mail he was creating evidence, and he would have phrased the e-mail with that in mind.

There's no magic to this. It's a matter of focus and discipline. E-mails must be written with the knowledge that they are not private and that they can live forever. If it will damage you, don't write it. If it will embarrass you, don't write it. Every time your fingers move to the keyboard, give yourself a private Miranda warning: everything you say can and will be held against you.

## Step Two: Knowing When to Document

Sometimes the risks will be obvious and the need for documentation will be plain—a customer has personally guaranteed to pay the balance owed by his company within thirty days in exchange for your agreement to ship more product; you've negotiated a hard-fought, crucial concession with the local zoning officer, and you can't afford to risk any misunderstanding; an employee with a disability has told you he wants no further accommodations; and so on.

But the most damaging "my word against your word" issues usually hide in the crevices of what seems like business as usual, camouflaged in normalcy, until it's too late. They arise from situations in which there were no apparent reasons to be on guard. These unforeseen battles—the ones that hit you when you least expect it, the ones you didn't plan for—are the ones that most often turn into the type of no-win litigation that can bring a business to its knees.

Every one of these hidden lawsuits-in-waiting that can be red flagged and neutralized before it gets started is money in your pocket.

### The "How Bad Will It Be if I Can't Prove What Just Happened?" Question

The difficulty is that you're not likely to spot a red flag unless you're looking for it, and understandably, most businesspeople don't focus on the negative. One of the key attributes of successful executives and entrepreneurs, in particular, is an unyielding optimism that gives them the motivation they need to fight through the roadblocks that would send negative thinkers packing.

Yet the fact is that, sometimes, positive thinking crosses a line and masks the foreseeable, tangible risks that a business needs to account for. Key employees leave. Banks pull lines of credit. Competitors steal important customers. Suppliers increase their prices. As valuable an entrepreneurial asset as it can be, when positive thinking moves too far in the direction of wishful thinking, it can interfere with the kind of preventive analysis and planning that truly successful businesses work into their operational fabric.

The solution is a middle ground: a hallmark of businesses that prosper over the long term is a leadership team that incorporates a *healthy pessimism* into their thinking—not a pessimism that threatens to overwhelm the optimism that drives business plans into business realities, but a parallel awareness of the risks and pitfalls that may present themselves. This mantra repeats throughout this book: You cannot avoid a risk unless and until you know it's there and you acknowledge its importance. Rose-colored glasses are fine, so long as they don't prevent you from seeing what needs to be seen.

This kind of healthy pessimism is a key, foundational attribute for anyone seeking to avoid "my word against your word" lawsuits. A healthy pessimist will ask himself this question as he moves through his business day: *"How bad will it be if I can't prove what just happened?"* He won't assume that things will always go right, any more than he would assume that things will always go wrong. Instead, he will focus on *what's at stake*—and if it's important, he'll then think about how to make sure he can prove it in the event of a dispute. A vendor offers a 10 percent discount on orders placed within sixty days. You're not planning on ordering anything significant within that time frame . . . not worth the trouble to document. You warn an employee that the failure to complete the report by the end of the month will be grounds for termination. You want to be able to prove that you gave that warning in case termination is necessary . . . document it. A minority partner agrees to accept a lower-profit percentage in exchange for your guarantee of a bank loan. That could turn into real money . . . document it. The project owner tells you to substitute a cheaper material than that shown on the plan. If he denies giving you that go-ahead later on, there could be real problems . . . document it. A software consultant tells you the work will be done in two weeks. You're not in that much of a hurry

> ⇢ **You cannot avoid a risk unless and until you know it's there and you acknowledge its importance. Rose-colored glasses are fine, so long as they don't prevent you from seeing what needs to be seen.**

and you'd rather he take his time . . . no need for documentation. When you're in the midst of a back-and-forth business communication, think about how damaging a potential disagreement over who said what might be. If it's worth worrying about, it's worth documenting.

> --> **When you're in the midst of a back-and-forth business communication, think about how damaging a potential disagreement over who said what might be. If it's worth worrying about, it's worth documenting.**

## The Trust Factor

Suppose you're dealing with someone you trust, someone you know to be completely honest? Do you still need to worry about documentation?

I do not believe that your trust in the other side should overwhelm your documentation decision. The fact that you trust a particular vendor, customer, contractor, employee, or consultant is relevant, but it should not be determinative.

"My word against your word" issues are not limited to instances in which a dishonest adversary twists the truth out of self-interest; often, they arise from honest, good-faith disagreements that spring from the foibles in human perception and memory. Psychological studies over many decades have documented in wide-ranging contexts how people who see or hear the same thing at the same time will honestly recall and report it in vastly different ways. People who see the same car accident routinely testify to vastly different versions of what happened. Experienced lawyers don't bat an eye when five reputable business executives testify under oath to five different versions of the same meeting. It happens all the time—humans are poor recording devices.

> --> **Good documents, like good fences, head off the kinds of disputes that ruin good relationships.**

Indeed, the fact that you respect and trust the person with whom you are making a deal is an excellent reason to make sure you document what you've agreed to. Good documents, like good fences, head off the kinds of disputes that ruin good relationships.

## Step Three: The Documentation Arsenal

Once you've decided that something is worth documenting, how do you do it? Here are the primary (not the only, but those I believe to be the most useful) options in the twenty-first-century documentation arsenal, starting with the least cumbersome and least reliable, and ending with the most cumbersome and most reliable.

1. Take notes or create a file memo.
2. Send a "confirming" e-mail.
3. Send a "response-demanded" e-mail.

### Notes and File Memos

Notes and files memos are easy to prepare, and can be powerful evidence—as Lucas Goode well knew. I have clients who keep notes on their circa-1960 paper desk calendars, which can work just fine. I have clients who type notes into a running Word document while they're on the telephone. That works as well. I have clients who carry state-of-the-art miniature recorders into which they dictate memos while driving between assignments. That works, too.

There's no one way to keep notes and memos, but there *are* some basic rules that will imbue them with increased credibility and that will improve the likelihood that they will be admissible in court, should it come to that.

1. *Get it down as it happens.* Notes and memos should be prepared as close in time to the events in question as possible—the less you depend on your memory, the better. Notes taken during a meeting or while talking on the telephone can be powerful evidence. But a memorandum dictated a day or two after the meeting presents some problems.

2. *Can you prove when you wrote it?* One of the problems with notes and memos is that, theoretically, they can be created years after the fact. When faced with a damning handwritten note or calendar

entry, a lawyer will try to cast doubt on its genuineness by pointing out how easy it would have been to create and backdate it after the need for documentation became known. One way to avoid this is by e-mailing yourself. Whether you're at your desk or on the road and using your PDA, an e-mail will be date-stamped. You can also create notes and memos on a word-processing system that sequentially numbers documents so they can be tied into a specific date. Another way to do it is to have another witness (for instance, your assistant) date and initial handwritten entries.

**3.** *Don't recopy or discard your notes.* Never recopy and then discard your original notes, even if you only intend to make them more legible or clear up ambiguities. Your original notes are the most credible—recopying raises the possibility that you changed the content. Similarly, do not dictate a memo and then discard the original handwritten notes on which it was based. You need to be able to prove that the memo was faithful to the notes. Don't worry about doodles and coffee stains on the notes—these show that you did not create something solely for courtroom purposes, and that can make them more credible.

⤳ **Never recopy and then discard your original notes, even if you only intend to make them more legible or clear up ambiguities . . . Don't worry about doodles and coffee stains on the notes— these show that you did not create something solely for courtroom purposes, and that can make them more credible.**

**4.** *Make taking notes and creating memos a part of your routine.* Documents that are specially created for a particular event are not nearly as credible as documents prepared as a part of your ordinary routine. You will be asked why you took notes or wrote a memo. Did you foresee trouble and wish to create a document that supported your side of the story? Did you create a special document just for this incident? If (like Lucas Goode) you routinely take notes or write memos as a part of your everyday business activities, you have a perfect answer: I always take notes and write memos, and in this situation, I was only doing what I always do.

**5.** *Be prepared to live with what you write.* As is the case with e-mails, when a lawsuit is commenced, your adversary will have an almost unfettered right to obtain copies of your notes, memos, and files. More than one major lawsuit has been turned upside down by an incriminating note or memo buried in a file. And just as often, what is *not* written down is as important as what appears on the page. If your position is that an assurance was given during a meeting, and if you took notes during that meeting and the assurance appears nowhere in your documentation, you will have a hard time proving your case. Live by the notes, die by the notes.

While notes and memos can be very useful, they are inherently susceptible to the argument that because they were created solely by you and never vetted or approved by the other side, you could have easily slanted the content to serve your interests—including what was good for you and excluding what was bad for you.

To address that issue, all of the other options in the documentation arsenal involve some form of *interactive* documentation that includes the other side in the process. Doing so creates an entirely different dynamic: rather than being a private enterprise, documentation becomes a joint enterprise among the parties transacting business, and in the process, the documents that are created become more credible and powerful.

The advent of e-mail as the default mode of business communication has made this interactive form of documentation practical and effective—so long as you know what you're doing, and so long as you apply certain disciplines to the process, as explained in the next two sections.

## The "Confirming" E-Mail

The most basic form of interactive documentation involves the "confirming" e-mail. It's the "here's the deal/tell me if I'm wrong" kind of e-mail that is as annoyingly prevalent as it is exceptionally useful.

To maximize the legal impact of a confirming e-mail, think about it in terms of three components.

First, there's the "Here's the deal" or "This is what happened" part. For instance, "I am writing to confirm your price quote of $10 per unit," or "I wanted to confirm your advice that you will vacate the premises on August 1." Obviously, in order for the confirming e-mail to have any real utility, this component must be accurate, complete, and free from ambiguity.

Second, there's the "I'm relying on you" part. This is often implicit, but the point is to make sure that the recipient knows you're depending on him to tell you if you've made a mistake. For instance, "We require this information so that we can determine if we need to find an alternative supplier," or "We need to verify the date so that we can advise the next tenant accordingly." This can have substantial legal significance. If the recipient doesn't respond despite knowing that you're going to take steps based on your belief that the e-mail is accurate, and only later claims that you misstated the facts in your e-mail, he will have a much tougher time trying to explain why he didn't say something sooner.

Finally, there is the "Tell me if I'm wrong" part. You should affirmatively ask that the recipient respond if your e-mail is wrong. "If I am incorrect, I request that you advise me immediately." You need to take away any possibility that the recipient will claim that he didn't know you wanted to hear from him if there were problems.

Your hope in sending a confirming e-mail is that the recipient will read it, assess it as a fair and accurate statement, and see no need to respond other than agreeably, if at all. If that's what happens, and if there is a subsequent dispute, you will have a solid argument that your version of the facts is correct—if not, you'll contend, the recipient should have said something.

If, however, the recipient does let you know that he disagrees with your e-mail, at least you'll know early on that you've got a problem, and you'll have the opportunity to either work out your differences through a further exchange of e-mails or part company before either side wastes time and money.

Had Owen Moore been thinking as a healthy pessimist, he would have realized what was at stake and dashed off a quick confirming e-mail to Lucas Goode right after their initial conversation:

> Lucas—Thanks for the order. I really appreciate it. As we discussed, I'll accept a 10 percent discount off our usual pricing and a six-month installment arrangement that will not begin until May so that most of your payments can be shifted into your next fiscal year. I know you'd like delivery in six weeks. I'll do my best, but our usual delivery time is twelve weeks, so I can't make any promises.
>
> I'm ordering the materials and processing the order on this basis. If you disagree with any of the above, please let me know immediately. Thanks again.

Think how much differently the dispute between Moore and Goode would have unfolded had Moore taken the five minutes it would have required to compose and send this confirming e-mail. If Goode had offered no objection to Moore's e-mail, their initial conversation would have proceeded down a wholly different path. "I sent you an e-mail explaining the status of the deal the same day we talked, Lucas. I told you I was moving forward on this basis. I asked you to tell me if you disagreed, and you said nothing. How is this my fault?" During his cross-examination, Moore would have been able to give Fairley a hefty dose of her own courtroom medicine. "I explained the deal in writing to your client the day it was made, Ms. Fairley. I asked him to tell me if I got anything wrong, and he never objected. He had time to make up an internal memo. Why didn't he have time to respond to me? We both know the answer to that, don't we, Ms. Fairley—he didn't object because he knew the e-mail was perfectly accurate."

The upshot is that had Moore spent the few minutes required to document the conversation through a short, quick confirming e-mail, it would have likely been Goode, not Moore, looking for an exit strategy.

There are, as there always are, some rules and cautions that must be kept in mind.

- You need to make sure you can prove the recipient received your confirming e-mail. Use an e-mail system that generates receipts, *and keep the receipts*. Software programs are available that will more reliably confirm delivery of an e-mail. Talk to your IT people or consultants.

- Make *sure* the e-mail says what you need it to say. This is an art, not a science, and depending on your experience and aptitude in this arena, the complexity and scope of the transaction, and a host of other factors, you might need some help with your content and phraseology. You might not know all the legal nuances of what you are getting into, and in some contexts, it's very easy to unwittingly create something that will ultimately explode in your face. (See "The Attorney Hotline" topic on page 34.)

- What do you do if you're the recipient of a confirming e-mail? First, recognize it for what it is—we are all awash in e-mails, but you *cannot* let these kinds of e-mails slip through the cracks. They won't necessarily announce themselves as e-mails of significance; sometimes, key confirmatory content is buried in gently worded small talk. Keep your antennae up. Review these e-mails carefully, and respond if there are misstatements or omissions. If you have any insecurity or if something doesn't smell right, get some help—again, see "The Attorney Hotline" suggestion.

## The "Response-Demanded" E-Mail

As useful as a confirming e-mail can be, it has one basic flaw: the recipient can deny ever having seen it. "That e-mail was all wrong. Maybe I got it, but I never saw it. I get a ton of e-mails, and I'm not perfect. If I had seen it, I would have responded right away, that's for sure." Believable? Maybe. Maybe not. That's the problem—a lack of certainty.

A "response-demanded" e-mail is designed to solve that problem. It is exactly the same as a confirming e-mail, except that instead of a "Please let me know if I'm wrong" component, it includes an "I ask that you confirm your agreement to the contents of this e-mail in writing" requirement.

This puts the onus on the sender to get a response. In the confirming e-mail context, no news is good news—silence is acquiescence. In the response-demanded e-mail context, however, no response means no agreement. The sender has to keep bugging the recipient to respond, one way or the other—until the response is received, everything is up in the air. But once the confirmatory response is received, the agreement or the representation or whatever else needs to be nailed down gets nailed down. An affirmative response to a response-demanded e-mail is the functional equivalent of a signed, written agreement.

> ⇢ **As useful as a confirming e-mail can be, it has one basic flaw: the recipient can deny ever having seen it . . . A "response-demanded" e-mail is designed to solve that problem.**

*Caution*: If you are using a response-demanded e-mail to confirm an agreement, beware of the "we agree, but . . ." response. In order to form a binding agreement, the law requires an offer and an *unconditional* acceptance of the offer. An acceptance with conditions, exceptions, or qualifications is not an acceptance—it's a counteroffer. "I agree to pay $10 per unit as quoted by you but only if payment terms are net 60" is a counteroffer. "I will commence this assignment on August 1 and charge a flat fee of $10,000 as you request, but will require a $5,000 retainer" is a counteroffer. You can turn the counteroffer into a binding agreement with your own unconditional acceptance, but until one side or the other gets to a simple and uncomplicated "agreed," there may be no deal.

This is another reason to have your attorney lurking in the background and whispering in your ear, as explained in "The Attorney Hotline" section. Sometimes, what seems simple is actually complex.

All of the other instructions and cautions that pertain to confirming e-mails apply to response-demanded e-mails as well.

WHETHER TO SEND ANY SORT of corroborating e-mail is a strategic, case-by-case decision. There is no denying that even a mildly worded confirming e-mail will cause the recipient to look more closely at what's being confirmed, and will thereby increase the odds that some objection will be raised. I suggest that it is almost always a good thing, not a bad thing—better you know now, not later, if there's going to be a problem. But maybe you have your reasons and would prefer to let the sleeping dog lie, gambling on the fact that it will never wake up. That can be a tough way to do business, but that's your call based on the circumstances.

Once the decision to engage in an interactive documentation process is made, however, e-mails (if properly managed) are the most advantageous method of communication in almost all contexts.

Conceptually, you can, of course, confirm agreements and events via a letter, and you can duplicate the speed of an e-mail by faxing or hand delivering the letter. But if there is a problem to be worked out, letters fall far short of what e-mails can accomplish. E-mails provide a real-time, almost effortless, near-conversational conduit for the exchange of arguments and ideas. That kind of instantaneous give-and-take leads to compromise—and the e-mail process (again, if properly managed, keeping the problems of unintentional documentation in mind) creates the kind of written record that stops "my word against your word" problems before they begin.

You could also confirm agreements and events and try to work out any resulting problems through a telephone conversation or a meeting, and particularly when the disagreements are deep or complicated, this might be the best course. E-mail is a wonderful tool, but sometimes an eye-to-eye conversation is better. Nevertheless, at the end of that road, you'll be right back where you started—in the breeding ground for a "my word against your word" dispute. You'll want to carefully document whatever agreement was ultimately struck, which means that you'll want to seriously consider using a confirming or response-demanded e-mail to make sure all parties are on the same page.

Once you decide that e-mail is the best course, the choices between a confirming e-mail and a response-demanded e-mail and of how informal, formal, friendly, or demanding to make them are strategic decisions based on experience and circumstances. If you can afford to take some chances, that will point you in one direction; if what's at stake is something you just can't chance at all, that will point you in a different direction; if the terms of the e-mail are complicated and detailed, that implicates still another style. Your expertise and the advice of a savvy lawyer (again, see "The Attorney Hotline" section) will be your best bet.

There's no denying that e-mail has had a revolutionary, shape-shifting effect on business communications, generally, and the documentation of business transactions, in particular. This can be celebrated or bemoaned, depending on your perspective. But it can't be ignored. The simple truth is that the failure to appreciate the benefits and apprehend the risks inherent in business e-mails is business malpractice.

## The Attorney Hotline

Business law and the legal system generally are replete with problematic and disconcerting realities. We've already discussed one of them at length: The truth does not always matter. In the eyes of the law, the only thing that really matters is what you can prove, and in the process, the truth can be turned inside out.

Here is another dose of counterintuitive reality: Your common sense and business judgment can get you into legal trouble. They're *dangerous*. Your common sense and business judgment probably have a great deal to do with what made you successful, but when it comes to the law and the management of legal risks, it is extremely risky to rely on what seems right. There's a reason why it takes three years to complete law school and probably another ten years of experience before an attorney starts to know what he's doing. There's a lot to know, and it's not instinctive. Chapter Two will make that painfully evident.

> ⟶ **Your common sense and business judgment probably have a great deal to do with what made you successful, but when it comes to the law and the management of legal risks, it is extremely risky to rely on what seems right.**

Here's the point: You *must* focus on documentation, but you need to make sure you're documenting the right thing, using the right words. Otherwise, your own words could be the weapon that defeats you. You cannot rely on gut feel for that.

Let's suppose you make a deal with a supplier. You need the materials in thirty days. To make sure he delivers, you make a deal over the phone, and you send him a confirming e-mail: "This confirms our deal—if the materials aren't here in thirty days, you will pay me a penalty of $50,000." Makes sense—it gives the supplier the incentive you want. But the penalty is most likely unenforceable. There's a whole body of law you probably don't know anything about that applies to these kinds of "liquidated damages" provisions, as they're called (the topic is discussed in more detail in Chapter Four). There were better ways to meet your goal that only an experienced lawyer would know.

Let's suppose you make a deal with certain nonexempt employees who typically work five, sometimes ten, hours of overtime a week. Instead of keeping track of all the hours and figuring out what to pay them, which is cumbersome and expensive, you agree to pay each of them for eight overtime hours a week even if they put in less than that. Some weeks they'll be overpaid; some weeks they'll be underpaid; but over the long term, they'll end up making more than they're entitled to, and you'll save administrative time and money. You duly document the agreement in a memo to each employee. It's a win-win, and the employees love it—except that it's illegal (you'll learn why in Chapter Two). Once the Department of Labor views your memos, you'll likely be subject to fines and penalties.

Let's suppose you make a deal with a consultant to design a logo for your stationery. You send a simple, confirming e-mail—here's what he will design, here's what he will charge. He comes up with a design that you love, and you ask him to send you the electronic file so you can put it on your Web site, emboss it on pens, cups, and other client giveaways, and so on. Not so fast, he says—I'm the one who owns the logo, not you, and I only agreed that you could use it on your stationery. Wait a second, you say, that makes no sense. I paid you to design this for me, and I get to do what I want with it. The fact is he has a solid position under the law—a good lawyer would have had you document what's known as a "work for hire" provision in the deal (explained in Chapter Three), but you didn't. He may well have you over a barrel.

One of your administrative assistants says he's developed carpal tunnel syndrome and arthritis, and he can't use his computer unless it's equipped with special equipment, including a voice recognition package. The cost will be upward of $2,000. You like him, but you know the other administrative assistants are going to be resentful if he receives special treatment. So, you tell him that you're willing to do this, but he's going to have to pay for it—$50 will be deducted from every paycheck until the equipment cost is covered. He says he can't afford to lose his job and reluctantly agrees. You confirm the deal in a letter. All is well until you receive the claim notice from the Equal Employment Opportunity Commission (EEOC)—what you did is a plain violation of the

Americans with Disabilities Act (ADA), as discussed in Chapter Two, and your letter is attached as Exhibit A.

There's no way you can know all of this. But there's no way you can do without this know-how and, at the same time, create the documentation you'll need to win the "my word against your word" battles that will permeate your business life.

The solution to this dilemma is the old adage that "an ounce of prevention is worth a pound of cure" or, rephrased for this purpose, a ten-minute e-mail exchange or telephone consultation with a savvy and trusted lawyer *now* is better than a five-year lawsuit *later*. This prescription applies not only to documentation issues, but also to the myriad of legalities that thread their way into all aspects of commerce—including the topics dealt with throughout this book. There's a lot you can and should do for yourself. But you also need a safety net, a method to get a quick insight or confirmation, on the fly.

> ⟶ **Every business needs to develop a "hotline" relationship with a lawyer who understands how to stop legal problems before they start. You'll have to pay for the lawyer's time, but if you have the right lawyer and you manage the relationship wisely, there are few more valuable investments.**

Every business needs to develop a "hotline" relationship with a lawyer who understands how to stop legal problems before they start. You'll have to pay for the lawyer's time, but if you have the right lawyer and you manage the relationship wisely, there are few more valuable investments. Lawyers who have spent years representing and advising a variety of businesses become business anthropologists of a sort—they have seen and studied how other companies have solved or failed to solve an array of basic business issues, and they can use for your benefit what they've learned from the experience and mistakes of others.

In order for a hotline relationship to work, however, you must involve your lawyer sooner, not later. The point of this kind of relationship is to avoid the "if only you had talked to me first" conversation that characterizes so many attorney-client meetings. If you have decided to send a confirming e-mail, and you have any insecurity as to how best to phrase it, have your lawyer be the ghostwriter. Ditto if you're answering a response-demanded e-mail. If you're developing a strategy, the communication has to be in the nature of "I'm thinking about doing this; what do you think?" *not* "Here's what I've done; what do you think?" If you're responding to events, it must be "This just happened; how do you think I should proceed?" *not* "This just happened; here's what I've already done."

At the same time, the lawyer has to reciprocate. For a hotline relationship to work, the attorney has to have a "do it now" personality—certain attorneys check their BlackBerry night and day; certain attorneys don't. You have to be confident that the lawyer will, if feasible, get back to you right away. The attorney has to deal with you in a way that makes you feel comfortable asking *any* question, even at the risk of sounding naive or ill informed. And, of course, the attorney has to have the kind of broad-based skill set that engenders your confidence. If the lawyer doesn't measure up, get another lawyer.

In most situations, the Attorney Hotline relationship will not be nearly as complicated or cumbersome as it may seem. Sometimes the attorney is going to have to take a couple steps back and do some legal research before he can answer. However, most businesses have the kinds of issues that fall into categories that repeat themselves, and before too long, a knowledge base and a history develop, making things much simpler. The consultant issues and customer claims you discussed with your lawyer last year will help him craft the contract clauses you can use to prevent similar problems next year. The e-mail text your lawyer drafted to confirm the pricing deal you make now will be the template for the pricing deal you make later. *All* businesses will have employee issues (as discussed in Chapter Two). Make sure your lawyer is conversant with employment law—the Americans with Disabilities Act (ADA), the Family and Medical Leave Act (FMLA), the Fair Labor Standards Act (FLSA), the Equal Pay Act (Title VII), and so on. Once your lawyer has helped you confront an employee's request for an ADA accommodation or an FMLA leave, you'll be that much further along when the next employee makes a similar request. The procedure you develop to head off one employee's FLSA issue will work for an array of other employees as well. Eventually, what seemed like difficult problems become simplified routines.

Many times a day, my colleagues and I will receive e-mails from the clients with whom we've established this kind of hotline relationship. It's extremely satisfying for us to be able to work behind the scenes to keep them out of trouble and help them achieve competitive advantages, and it's extremely satisfying for them to have a resource to help them through the legal traps and pitfalls they know are there but can't quite identify.

Often, the e-mail or telephone contact is an "I don't think this is a problem, but I just wanted to check" message. Sometimes, what the client explains *is* a problem, and we have the opportunity to minimize it. Often, we'll receive a draft of a confirming or response-demanded e-mail for our review. We'll be able to work in the background without the other side knowing a lawyer is involved to change the phraseology in a way that favors our client. We'll also be able to point out when crucial issues aren't covered by the e-mail, and we'll be able to suggest workarounds. We'll ask questions the client might not have considered. Sometimes we'll tell the client that a confirming or response-demanded e-mail won't work, and he has to handle the matter in a more formal, written agreement. Sometimes we won't have to do anything at all.

I am not suggesting that you *should* make your lawyer your de facto business partner. Lawyers cost money. Carefully define who is authorized to request legal advice. Focus your consultations, and insist that your lawyer focus his advice, on the legal issues that matter the

⋯⟶ **I am not suggesting that you *should* make your lawyer your de facto business partner. Lawyers cost money. Carefully define who is authorized to request legal advice. Focus your consultations, and insist that your lawyer focus his advice, on the legal issues that matter the most.**

most. It's not always easy for nonlawyers to understand what those issues look like. Many of them are highlighted in the following chapters, and depending on the nature of your business, some preliminary "what kinds of issues should I be looking for" lawyer-client meetings could pay dividends. However, once you see one of those issues heading at you, you do need to make sure that you deal with it—really deal with it—before you lose the opportunity to keep it from spinning out of control. Think of it this way: You might not head for your mechanic every time your car has a rattle or squeak, but you know that having a mechanic check out the flashing red warning light on your dashboard now is a better alternative than letting things slide and risking engine failure in a couple of weeks. When there's a lot at stake, it's worth spending some time and money sooner to lessen the odds that you'll have to spend a whole lot more time and money later.

Your business and your career work the same way, except it's a lot harder to find the warning light, and if you let things get out of hand, the problems are a lot harder to fix.

## *Warning*: It Won't Work if You're the Only One Who Does It

One final bit of real world advice . . .

Let's suppose you run a manufacturing business and that, more than anything else, your profit margin depends on the cost of your raw materials. So, you send an e-mail to your purchasing agents: no one is authorized to buy more than $10,000 of raw materials unless you first approve the deal. One of your new purchasing agents, eager to impress and certain he's negotiated a great price, ignores your e-mail and signs an agreement for $100,000 of raw materials to be delivered in three months. In fact, the bottom is falling out of the market, and he got taken. Not to worry . . . you call the supplier and tell him that the purchasing agent was not authorized to sign the agreement, and you show him the e-mail to prove it. Are you OK?

No, you're not. You're stuck.

A fundamental, but often misunderstood, principle of business law known as "apparent agency" is the root of the problem. The upshot of the apparent agency doctrine is this: even if an employee is not authorized to make a commitment on behalf of a company, if it reasonably appears to the outside world that he is authorized, the company is stuck with the commitments that employee makes. So, for instance, if they haven't been told otherwise, suppliers can assume that an employee who holds the title purchasing agent can make purchasing deals. A vice president of a company would ordinarily be cloaked with the authority to make almost any kind of deal on behalf of a company. In business, books can be judged by their covers.

⇢ **The upshot of the apparent agency doctrine is this: even if an employee is not authorized to make a commitment on behalf of a company, if it reasonably appears to the outside world that he is authorized, the company is stuck with the commitments that employee makes.**

In practice, the rule makes a lot of sense. Think what would happen to your ability to conduct business if every time you dealt with someone from another company you would first have to obtain a written certification that he's authorized to deal with you. That's just not the way commerce functions, especially in the fast-paced, I-want-it-now, e-mail-dominated world most companies have to confront.

Yet there's an obvious downside. Because of the apparent agency doctrine, the "my word against your word" problem can afflict a wide array of a company's employees. You have to worry about much, much more than what you do or what upper management or department heads do. One of your customers claims that a sales representative granted a significant pricing discount, and the sales representative denies it. Or a subcontractor says your brand-new assistant vice president extended a performance deadline, and the assistant vice president denies it. Perhaps a consultant claims your receivables manager committed to a $25,000 cash-flow management-consulting deal, and the manager denies it. Whether these employees had the *actual* right to make these deals doesn't matter. The point is that, authorized or not, they can make deals and commitments that will stick because of their *apparent* authority, and if their opposite number wins the "my word against your word" battle, you're on the hook. In order to protect yourself, you must make certain that an appreciation of the "my word against your word" issue, and the documentation procedures required to overcome it, moves beyond top management and is actually adopted and utilized on a day-to-day basis by anyone who has the actual or apparent right to make decisions affecting customers, suppliers, employees, consultants, pricing, terms, specifications, deadlines . . . and anything else of significance.

⇢ **In order to protect yourself, you must make certain that an appreciation of the "my word against your word" issue, and the documentation procedures required to overcome it, moves beyond top management and is actually adopted and utilized on a day-to-day basis by anyone who has the actual or apparent right to make decisions affecting customers, suppliers, employees, consultants, pricing, terms, specifications, deadlines . . . and anything else of significance.**

You can't do that just by edict or through memos and manuals or through forms and procedures (though that's part of it). Training reinforced on an annual basis is the key. There's no other way to insinuate the right kind of insight and documentation methods into all pertinent levels of a company's culture and keep it there.

Depending on the size of the organization, the training can be done by outside experts, or by in-house personnel who have themselves been trained by the outside experts. The training can be completed in person, or it can be completed through "Webinars" or other e-learning methods. It has to be done, and it has to be done regularly. In addition, upper management should participate in and, then itself comply with, the protocols. I get a very different response when I train an organization in which upper management is an active and committed participant—actions speak louder than words.

Converting the right theories into actual practice is never easy, but that's what successful businesses do. Otherwise, it's all just talk.

Being the best candidate with the best ideas is important. But to really accomplish anything, you have to win the election. It's important to assemble the best players and the best coaches. All that really matters is who wins the game, not who looks good on paper. The same is true in business—Pyrrhic victories don't do much for the balance sheet. It's important to tell the truth and to do the right thing. At the end of the day, if you can't *prove* you told the truth and did the right thing, you'll have a clear conscience, but not much else.

There are certain things you *have* to do in order to become and stay successful. Winning the documentation war is one of them.

# CHAPTER TWO

# The Second Mistake: Losing the Employee vs. Employer War

THAT'S RIGHT. An employee vs. employer *war*.

Let's get this straight, up front. I'm not saying that the majority of your employees are plotting against you or that you should be plotting against them. I'm not saying that you should forgo efforts to treat your workforce fairly and expect the same in return or that efforts to motivate and forge partnerships with your employees will be fruitless or counterproductive. Much the opposite: an employee-employer relationship based on goodwill and good faith pays immense dividends—less litigation being one of them.

What I *am* saying is this: through a series of legislative and judicial actions at the federal, state, and local levels, employees have been equipped with a startling array of legal weapons they can use to bring claims against their employers that can be worth buckets of money—way into six and even seven figures—often for reasons that you could not have foreseen or imagined. Employees are taking advantage of the right to bring these claims with increasing frequency and success, some for valid reasons, some for opportunistic and manufactured

> ⇢ Through a series of legislative and judicial actions at the federal, state, and local levels, employees have been equipped with a startling array of legal weapons they can use to bring claims against their employers that can be worth buckets of money—way into six and even seven figures— often for reasons that you could not have foreseen or imagined.

reasons. Aside from the potentially debilitating damage awards, these claims can be hugely expensive to defend, they can result in embarrassing publicity, they are distracting and time-consuming, and they are corrosive to company morale. A few claims of this nature can eat a business alive. Employers *are* under attack, and ignoring or minimizing these threats is a huge and potentially fatal mistake.

Consider the numbers published by the Equal Employment Opportunity Commission (EEOC), the government agency that handles a substantial number of employee vs. employer issues. According to the EEOC, there was an astounding increase in employee vs. employer claims between 2006 and 2007. No one was certain whether the increase was a temporary spike or a trend—and then the number of claims increased *another* 15 percent in 2008. Consider: Age-discrimination claims were up 15 percent in 2007, and then increased an astounding, additional 29 percent in 2008. Gender-based claims were up 7 percent in 2007 (the highest number of claims since 2002) and increased another 14 percent in 2008. Race-discrimination claims rose 12 percent in 2007 (the highest number of claims since 1994) and climbed another 11 percent in 2008. Retaliation claims were up 18 percent in 2007 (an all-time record level) and increased yet another 23 percent in 2008. ADA claims rose 14 percent in 2007 (the highest number of claims since 1998) and climbed 10 percent in 2008. National-origin claims swelled by 12 percent in 2007 (the second highest number of claims ever) and increased another 13 percent in 2008. Religious-discrimination claims rose to 13 percent in 2007 (the highest number of claims ever) and rose again to 14 percent in 2008. Pregnancy-discrimination claims were up 14 percent in 2007 (the highest number of claims ever) and climbed another 12 percent in 2008 . . . and so on.

What does this mean in terms of dollars? The EEOC, during an administration not known for an employee-friendly approach, recovered $345 million from employers in 2007, *up 26 percent in one year*—and then increased that total to $376 million in 2008. These numbers only cover government litigation, which is a minor piece of the pie. According to Jury Verdict Research, a company that monitors damage awards, in 2001 the average award in privately litigated employment practices lawsuits (the vast majority of such lawsuits) was $435,562. In 2006, it rose to $683,828. In 2007, the average was $887,478—*up more than $200,000 in just one year.*

## Why Is Congress Allowing This to Happen?

Congress, along with state and local lawmaking bodies, generally views the employee vs. employer war as good news. There's no outcry among legislators to limit the right of employees to sue employers; compare the legislative efforts to reduce the frequency with which patients sue doctors or consumers sue product manufacturers. In fact, Congress wants to *increase* the number of employee vs. employer claims—in the last several years, for example, the Supreme Court issued decisions that made it more difficult for employees to bring certain kinds of claims against their employers. Congress's response was to amend the laws to negate what the Supreme Court had done—all to make it easier than ever for employees to successfully sue employers for more and more money.

The reason for this is policy-driven. Our government wants to prohibit certain kinds of workplace conduct. It has, therefore, passed a menagerie of laws that outlaw such conduct—sexual harassment, various types of prohibited discrimination, failure to pay overtime, denial of certain unpaid-leave requests, and so on. But passing a law takes with it the obligation to ferret out violations and enforce the law—a nightmarish proposition given the number and scope of workplaces across the nation. So, instead, the government has, in effect, outsourced the responsibility to find and punish offending employers to the nation's employees. In order to get those employees to accept the assignment, the government had to make it worth their while. And that's just what the government did.

# Employee vs. Employer Lawsuits:
# Little Risk, Lots of Reward

Here's how it works: In almost all legal contexts, if a plaintiff sues a defendant, the plaintiff bears his own legal fees. Typically, that means that either the plaintiff pays a lawyer by the hour or the lawyer takes a percentage of the eventual recovery if there is one (an arrangement known as a contingent fee). That has the healthy, free-market effect of winnowing borderline claims out of the system—a plaintiff will generally not be willing to write checks to a lawyer if the plaintiff is most likely going to lose or recover only a small amount, and a lawyer is not going to take a case on a contingent fee basis unless he's quite sure that he's going to win enough money to justify his time.

That's not, however, what happens in most employee vs. employer cases—the rules, and the results that typically follow from the rules, have been skewed.

Employees have the right to file certain kinds of claims with certain government agencies, most notably the EEOC, the Department of Labor (DOL), and the Department of Justice (DOJ). Those agencies have the responsibility to investigate the claims and decide if they wish to pursue them. During the investigation, they will generally run the employer through an expensive wringer, and if they ultimately think a case is worth pursuing, they will bring a lawsuit against the employer—all at taxpayer expense, all at no cost to the employee. The employee has all of the upside and none of the downside.

More often, however, the EEOC, DOL, and DOJ conclude that the cases they are asked to investigate are not sufficiently straightforward and clear-cut, and they opt not to pursue them further. In addition, there are many kinds of employee vs. employer claims that are not channeled through these agencies. In these instances, the employee has to decide if he wants to pursue the case on his own—but that decision won't be subject to the same kind of "Is this really a worthwhile claim?" financial analysis that applies to the rest of the litigation world. Not even close.

Unlike a normal lawsuit, if an employee wins a garden-variety harassment, discrimination, or similar claim against his employer, the law requires not only that the employer pay whatever damages the employee is awarded, but *also* that the employer pay the employee's lawyer. Winning can be a relative term: an employee might seek $500,000 from an employer, and "win" only $25,000 or less—practically speaking, a victory for the employer. In many situations, however, the law considers that a "win" for the employee, and the employer will *still* be required to pay *all* the reasonably justifiable legal fees the employee's lawyer can convince a judge to award, which can easily be $100,000, $200,000, or much more.

These awards have a huge, real world effect on employee vs. employer litigation. Because the vast majority of these kinds of employee vs. employer cases are handled pursuant to contingent fee agreements, the employee risks *nothing* for the privilege of taking a shot at his employer. From the employee's perspective, once again—all upside, no downside.

Still, the employee has to find a willing lawyer, and that's where the laws that require the employer to pay the employee's counsel fees come in. In a normal contingent fee case, a lawyer will be paid something in the range of one-third of the eventual recovery. If a lawyer believes, for instance, that it could consume $150,000 of his time to handle a hotly contested case to conclusion, he will probably refuse to accept the case unless he thinks he can obtain at least a $450,000 recovery. However, in the world of employee vs. employer cases, the lawyer could still get his $150,000 fee even if he only obtains, say, a $25,000 recovery—so long as he pulls off a technical "win," he gets paid. Economic reality has been removed from the equation. There's no linkage between the degree of success and the degree of compensation. Essentially, Congress and many local and state legislatures encourage employees (and lawyers who represent employees) to sue employers so that employees will, in effect, enforce employment laws in the workplace.

This *has* produced the desired result. Employers who violate employment laws are frequently and justifiably made to pay for it—big time. The word spreads, and the deterrent effect multiplies. More and more, smart, informed employers have implemented the measures required to comply with the law and minimize potential violations. That's all for the good.

→ Essentially, Congress and many local and state legislatures encourage employees (and lawyers who represent employees) to sue employers so that employees will, in effect, enforce employment laws in the workplace.

But there is an egregiously unfair downside to all of this. An attorney representing an employee can knowingly file a borderline-bogus suit, start some negotiations with the employer's attorney, and ultimately make the following pitch:

"You know what, you might be right. You probably have a much better chance at winning this lawsuit than I do," he'll say. "But, we both know that juries do funny things. If you don't win the suit outright, all I have to do is win just a fraction of what I'm after, and then your client will be stuck with my $150,000 bill for legal fees. My client's going to look awfully sympathetic on the witness stand. The jury's going to give him *something*, even if it's just a token. Are you willing to take the risk? Be smart. Pay me $50,000 now, and it's over."

The pitch is all dressed up in a suit and tie, but it's still remarkably similar to a not-so-subtle solicitation for "protection" money worthy of *The Sopranos*.

Sometimes the ploy works, and the employer pays what it considers to be legally extorted blood money. Sometimes it doesn't, and the employer digs in, plays hardball, and takes its chances. But it works often enough to have spawned a large and growing industry—lawyers who specialize in suing employers, some for good and justifiable reasons, others . . . not so much. Check the Yellow Pages under "Attorneys"—alongside page after page of "no fee unless we recover" ads seeking injured persons willing to file lawsuits, you'll find similar ads seeking employees willing to file lawsuits against their employers. There's a reason for that. There are hundreds of thousands of lawyers trying to make a living. They will follow the money.

A lot of social good can, and does, come from a process in which lawyers and clients seek each other out to right bona fide wrongs. Many employee vs. employer claims are fully justifiable and promote better and safer workplaces.

In the employee vs. employer world, however, the artificial imbalance in leverage and the disconnect between risk and reward have also fomented a noxious and socially destructive consequence: there is a growing mountain of lawsuits in which employees and their lawyers see the realistic potential to alchemize questionable claims into new cars and Caribbean vacations through extortionate demands. So why not, they reason, give it a try? The current state of employment law *does* encourage and propagate a monumental number of counterfeit claims, and because of that, the business community *is* in the throes of a debilitating and unjust employee vs. employer war it cannot afford.

> ⇢ The current state of employment law *does* encourage and propagate a monumental number of counterfeit claims, and because of that, the business community *is* in the throes of a debilitating and unjust employee vs. employer war it cannot afford.

My message is simple: you need to prevent these claims before they happen, and to the extent you cannot, you need to win them.

## Understanding the Problem:
## The "How Was I Supposed to Know *That*?" Issue

Employment law exists largely to compel employers to treat employees the way the government thinks employees should be treated.

Sometimes, thankfully, employment law mirrors and implements our fundamental and shared national values. For example, both culturally and legally we disdain racial discrimination and religious oppression. Consequently, it comes as no surprise to anyone who owns or manages a business that racial and religious discrimination are prohibited in the workplace. That's at the root of who we are.

Sometimes, though, employment law reflects what the government—more accurately, those in power at a particular time—would like our fundamental and shared national values *to become*.

This, too, can serve a supremely valuable social purpose. Workplace practices we now regard as barbaric were, not that long ago, completely legal and accepted as "That's just the way it is"—sweatshops, child labor, toxic work environments, seventy-hour (or more) workweeks, rampant discrimination, pervasive sexual harassment, and so on. Government intervened and, often against substantial resistance, effectuated a variety of legal (and, ultimately, cultural) changes that, at the time, were viewed by many as radical (yes, even socialist) intrusions into free enterprise.

However, sometimes government goes too far and, rather than focusing on the greater good, panders to employees as a voting bloc or legislatively imposes the ideology of a transient political majority.

··→ **For employers, business-as-usual things you've always done, things you wouldn't think twice about doing—things that make common sense—now create unforeseen legal consequences.**

Either way, whether well intentioned or politically intentioned, when government enacts laws in the effort to change the norms of the workplace, an uncoupling is frequently created between the law and those responsible for implementing the law—employers. The law and common sense no longer align; in fact, common sense can lead an employer astray.

For employers, business-as-usual things you've always done, things you wouldn't think twice about doing—things that make common sense—now create unforeseen legal consequences.

The problem in employment law, even more than in many other areas of law, becomes the "How was I supposed to know *that*?" response it so often provokes after a well-meaning business owner or manager is slammed with a costly and embarrassing employee claim. Employment law is a world replete with frustration and cognitive dissonance for employers. In this topsy-turvy legal universe, those who try their best to do the right thing often find themselves incredulously liable for having done the wrong thing.

The root of this conundrum lies in the fact that managing a business is a bottom-line endeavor: success is measured by the amount of profit achieved. Those who own or run a business reflexively and routinely assess their decisions against this standard; within established norms, that which generates profit is good, and that which reduces profit is bad. Many employment laws are financially counterintuitive—rather than rewarding profitability, these laws mandate that a business owner or manager do something that *reduces* profitability. Sometimes, the problem is a matter of the employer simply not knowing the rules have changed or not understanding what the rule changes mean in practice. Sometimes, it's a rule change being wholly counterintuitive and, from an employer's perspective, counterproductive and unjustifiable. Either way, the employer becomes trapped.

Consider laws (discussed later in this chapter) that require the retention of employees who can't perform all aspects of their job or that prohibit employers from firing employees who make questionable claims or that require employers to hold positions open for employees who insist on taking leaves of absence or that restrict the kinds of questions typically asked during employment interviews or that bar managers from firing employees who proselytize for unionization. There are good and justifiable reasons for many of these laws, but that will provide little solace to a manager whose career depends on maximizing profits and who unwittingly and innocently violates one of these laws in the cause of doing his job. When he pays the price—ranging from embarrassment to termination—he'll inevitably and understandably ask the "How was I supposed to know *that*?" question. Most business owners and managers aren't lawyers. How are they to know that there's some arcane law that converts what has always been standard practice into a potential lawsuit? The chasm between what employers need to know and what they can realistically know will not change for the better in the foreseeable future. On the contrary, the astonishing magnitude and breadth of the legislative, regulatory, judicial, and agency activity in the employment law field will continue to exacerbate the "How was I supposed to know *that*?" issue.

--→ **The chasm between what employers need to know and what they can realistically know will not change for the better in the foreseeable future. On the contrary, the astonishing magnitude and breadth of the legislative, regulatory, judicial, and agency activity in the employment law field will continue to exacerbate the "How was I supposed to know *that*?" issue.**

Much of this activity is fomented by the natural forces that animate our local, state, and national politics. The country is comprised of tens of millions of employees who work for hundreds of thousands of employers. Employees and employers comprise a huge segment of those who vote, make campaign contributions, and support the lobbyists who skillfully assault lawmakers in the quest for legislative and regulatory enactments. Elected officials in the executive and legislative branches, from city halls and town councils to the White House and Congress, cannot achieve or maintain office without currying favor with one side or the other, and that keeps employment law in a perpetual governmental spotlight. Changes in the law naturally flow with the ebb and tide of election cycles: Democrats and Republicans usually have substantially different employment law platforms, and when one party replaces another, locally or nationally, it implements new legislative and regulatory enactments in the effort to satisfy its campaign promises and its ideological agendas.

The judicial branch also contributes to the onslaught of employment law activity. As mentioned previously, thousands of employee vs. employer claims are brought by government agencies and by lawyers representing employees, spurred on by legislation encouraging these lawsuits. These cases result in volume upon volume of judicial decisions. Some of those decisions are meant to explain what the legislative and regulatory enactments mean in practice; other decisions are meant to define the procedural requirements that must be followed in the employment law universe; and, often, different judges consider the same issues and reach different conclusions.

These processes feed and build upon themselves, resulting in an intertwined, layered, multipronged, ever-expanding, and often incongruous and ambiguous body of laws, regulations, and rulings, consuming hundreds upon hundreds of thousands of pages, all of which we generically call employment law.

Click through the federal government's efforts to explain some of it at www.eeoc.gov and www.dol.gov. Take a look at the Society for Human Resources Management Web site at www.shrm.org. Type *employment law* or *employee rights* into a search engine. You'll quickly see the enormity of the subject. Pick out some pages at random and read them. Odds are, in a minute or two, you'll be asking yourself, "How was I supposed to know *that*?"

Another factor will even further complicate life for employers. The Obama administration and the Democratic leadership in Congress have promised an array of legislative changes that will make it even easier (and more profitable) for employees to sue employers, and personnel changes at the EEOC, the DOL, and the DOJ will ensure more aggressive enforcement activities in the employment practices field.

Still, all is not hopeless; there *are* solutions. But before we get there, it is vitally important to understand how these issues arise. The solutions will make more sense once you understand the problem.

---

## The Case of Equal Employment Opportunity Commission, et al. vs. Moore Company and Owen Moore

Noah Ford, Owen Moore's longtime chief financial officer, scheduled a meeting with Moore as soon as the Goode Manufacturing trial ended.

"Come on in, Noah. You look worried."

"It's that obvious?"

"It is. And if you're worried, I suppose I should be worried. What's up?"

"I know you've been tied up with this lawsuit, Owen. But we need to talk numbers. Business is off. Way off. A lot of it is due to the economy, I'm sure. But whatever the reason might be, the fact is that our cash flow stinks. And on top of everything else, there's this Goode Manufacturing settlement. I've run all the scenarios I can think of, and I'm not sure how we're going to make it."

"I've looked at the same reports you've looked at, Noah, and I'm just as concerned as you are. But this is when managers earn their keep. We'll get through this."

"Easier said than done, Owen. We need to find a way to cut our costs and increase our productivity right now. Not next month. Now."

"I get it, Noah. I really do. I've considered our options, and they all point in one direction. We can't do anything about our building—we're locked into a lease. Our bank's not going farther out on a limb with us in this economy. I can try to negotiate with our suppliers, but I did that last year, and I don't think that'll go anywhere. We could raise our prices, but in this economy I don't want to give our customers another incentive to look at our competition."

"I can see where this is going."

"There's only one option left, Noah—our employees. We have to cut workforce costs and raise workforce productivity at the same time. Otherwise, in six to ten months, there won't be a workforce."

Moore and Ford spent the next week analyzing each department in Moore Company—Administration (twenty employees), Design (fifteen employees), Production and Distribution (eighty employees), and Sales and Marketing (fifteen employees). Moore and Ford then met with the four department managers.

Moore began the meeting by handing out a graph that plotted projected receipts against projected costs over the next twelve months. After three months, the receipts and costs lines started to periodically intersect, and after six months, costs consistently exceeded receipts. "Take a look at this. It says all there is to say."

He had their attention.

"Here's the plan. This will not be easy or pleasant. But your job and, for that matter, my job depend on this. We need to cut the amount we spend on wages and benefits and increase the amount of productivity we get from our employees. I want you to know that we considered every other option. There are no other viable alternatives."

Ford began to unfold a spreadsheet.

Moore went on, "One option is to keep the workforce we have and cut wage and benefit rates, maybe go to a four-day week, but Noah and I don't think that will work as well as a reduction in force. We think the best strategy is to cut employees and ask more from the people we retain. They'll be looking over their shoulders, knowing they could be the next to go, and they'll give us the productivity we need at a lower overall cost. Noah has the numbers. Noah?"

Ford read from his spreadsheet. "Administration needs to reduce to fifteen employees. Design needs to go to twelve employees. Production and Distribution, you have to cut to sixty employees. Sales and Marketing stays the same, but we change the compensation structure—we reduce the salary and increase the commission rate."

Moore stood up. He had rehearsed this. He usually tried to lighten up his department-manager meetings with some humor and backslapping. This time, however, he intentionally kept the meeting as somber and serious as he could make it. He did not smile. No small talk. Moore understood that the department managers would not like what had to be done, and he had to let them know that they had no choice. It had to be conveyed as a "do it and do it well—or else."

"Look. I know this is all easier said than done. But this is what managers do. I'm convinced we can get through this by cutting the least valuable people, by combining some job functions, and by coaching and cajoling the employees we retain to produce more and better work. You will need to bring all your skills to the table to make this happen."

Heads nodded.

"Develop your plan within the next three days. Schedule a meeting with Noah to fine-tune it. I want a final plan from each of you, in writing, on my desk within one week. No excuses. We'll then meet individually and go over it. You will then proceed with implementation. Any questions?"

They got the message. There were no questions.

Moore met first with the department manager for Production and Distribution, Florence Charte. "Flo, I understand the difficulty of what I've asked you to do—cut a full quarter of your team. I've reviewed your plan. Thanks for being so detailed."

"As I said in my memo, there's only one way I can get this done, Owen. If I am going to cut one-quarter of the people and still get the same amount done, the people who are left in Production and Distribution have to be people who can get one-quarter more done in the same amount of time. So, I used that as my criteria and made my cuts on that basis."

"Let's go over this employee by employee just to make sure I understand. Tell me about this first group you described in your memo."

"The first thing I did was review absentee records for the last two years. Attendance in my department has been generally excellent, but there are four people who took several weeks of unpaid leave because of medical issues, and another two who took a substantial amount of unpaid leave to care for a sick kid or parent. I sympathize, but this might be a recurring issue with these folks, and I won't be able to afford this kind of absenteeism. I can't take a chance. They're the first to go."

"Understood. Tell me about the next group."

"I've got two employees with a medical history that scares me. One of them had disk surgery a year ago. He's been fine since then, but same deal, I can't take the chance of a relapse. Another has a heart condition. She says it's controlled by medication, and she hasn't missed any time, but that's another chance I can't take if we have to make these cuts. If I've got to choose between someone who has obvious potential health issues and someone who doesn't . . ."

"I get it. Makes sense."

"I've got one guy who's got a bad knee and can't get up the stairs. He had to carry supplies up the stairs once or twice a day, and I assigned another employee to do that for him, just to give him a break. I won't have that luxury anymore, so he's got to go. I've got another employee who spends 80 percent of his time as a dispatcher, but every so often I need him to fill in on the loading dock. Several months ago, he told me he can't lift more than ten pounds. I can't afford a guy with limited capabilities, and I'll replace him with someone who can do both functions."

"OK."

"Also in that general category, I've got two employees who are pregnant. I can't afford to have them out for maternity leave and I can't afford the 'I've got a sick baby' absenteeism I know I'm going to get once they return to the job. There's more risk with them than with others, so I have to let them go."

"Understood."

"But, Owen, I just can't cut them off. They don't have a shot at getting another job until they deliver, and they won't be able to start looking seriously for six weeks thereafter. I'd like to pay them a month's severance and continue their benefits through the delivery and for three months afterward. I know we're strapped for cash, Owen, but there's a human side to this."

"OK. I need to sleep, too."

"There are also a few other women who want to start families soon. At least that's been the scuttlebutt. That means more maternity leave. So, I'm going to have to put them on the cut list, too."

"Got it. Tell me about the others."

"Two employees have been here forever and are set in their ways. They won't do well if they're given extra job duties. Plus, they're fifty or older, and I doubt if they have the energy to do what we're going to need. I've got to make this department younger if we're going to pull this off."

"OK. Keep going."

"I've got a couple of complainers in the department. Morale will be crucial—everyone's going to be working harder. The majority of these people will suck it up and not make a big deal out of it. However, there are a couple that I think will be really negative, and that could hurt. You know them."

"Who are they?"

"One of them was passed over for the lead foreman job and claimed it was because he is black. Remember he filed an EEOC Complaint? Even the EEOC saw it was bogus, and they dismissed it. He's been angry at everything and everyone ever since."

"That did upset me. We don't discriminate here, and we were vindicated. That guy had no business trying to play the race card. Who else?"

"The other is that woman who complained about supposed sexual harassment. You remember that?"

"I do remember. What a tempest in a teapot. I told Lou Case to deal with you on that, didn't I?"

"You did. But he saw things differently than you. No offense, Owen, but that guy does not understand the real world sometimes."

"Let's hear it."

"You know I won't stand for sexual harassment in my department, Owen. Those days are over. But I also won't stand for women who don't know the difference between sexual harassment and some harmless, good-natured fun. This isn't a tea room. It's a factory. Women are never going to be seen as equals in this kind of place unless they can handle some razzing, even if it's off-color. Whatever was said to her was no worse than what the guys say to each other every day. It was no big deal. In my book, that's not sexual harassment."

"What was her gripe?"

"She told me she wasn't used to that kind of language and that she couldn't take it. I told her she needed to get used to it. She didn't like that, so she complained to you, and you let Lou Case know about it."

"What did Lou say? I never heard anything more about it."

"He said we should issue some reprimands and tell the guys to knock it off. Make her happy. Damn, that kind of approach sets women back. I know harassment, and this wasn't it. If men feel they've got to treat women like delicate flowers, we're never going to get anywhere."

"So how did it turn out?"

"Just like I told your genius lawyer it would. I met with the guys and told them to cut it out. They were *not* happy. I lost some trust in that bargain. And there's been a lot of ill will ever since. So now they stay away from her. Before, she complained because they treated her like one of the guys. Now she complains because they *don't* treat her like one of the guys."

"I know the type."

"Anyhow, she's walking around with a face you wouldn't believe. I don't know if she's going to sue us, quit, sabotage, something. I just don't trust her."

"That's just more trouble than it's worth. I agree, Flo. Make all this happen."

Moore then met with the remaining department managers. The Administration Department manager reasoned that because most of his people were tied to their computers, he could judge their productivity by seeing how much computer time they spent on company business, as opposed to personal. He pulled each employee's e-mail account and read sent and received e-mails. Those who had the greatest volume of nonwork-related e-mails were judged to be the least committed to the job and were put on the termination list.

The Design Department manager explained that the design function was highly collaborative—all the designers had to work closely together. In recent months, politics seemed to dominate their conversations. Most leaned toward the liberal viewpoint, but two were staunch conservatives. Both sides were aggressively outspoken, and some heated, even vituperative exchanges had left a residual tension in the department. Another designer was a devout Muslim who emigrated from Iraq shortly after 9/11. Designers would occasionally work directly with customers, and a few customers refused to work with the Muslim designer. As one put it, "Why should I work with someone whose relatives could be terrorists, when I can just as easily work with an American?" All other things being equal in terms of qualifications and work ethic, the minority group of conservatives and the Muslim designer were cut in the interest of departmental harmony and customer satisfaction.

"Alright, here's how we're going to do it." Ford had convened a meeting of the department managers to establish a procedure to implement the terminations. "Let's not make this any more painful than it has to be. Call them in around lunchtime on Friday. Tell them they've been laid off due to economic conditions and leave it at that. Give them the rest of the day to pack up and say their good-byes."

"What if they ask why they were selected for the layoff as opposed to someone else?" Charte asked. "You know that's going to come up."

"There's no upside to getting into that. Just tell them management made some judgment calls based on what they felt was best for the company, and you're not authorized to say anything else."

Lois Price, the Sales and Marketing Department manager, raised her hand. "Noah, as you know, we're not making any cuts, but we are changing the salary and commission arrangement. How do we implement that?"

"Thanks for reminding me. Owen and I have drafted a memo to the sales force. I'll e-mail it to you. It will come from you and simply say that due to economic conditions, a new salary-and-commission structure will go into effect on the first of the month. If you are hit with questions or complaints, tell them this wasn't your call, and if they feel they can't operate under the new system, they're free to leave, no hard feelings. It won't be hard finding replacements in this economy. We simply have no choice."

The termination meetings went as might have been expected. Some employees said little. Some responded with anger and accusations. Some cried.

■　■　■

Three months into the Moore Company Rescue Plan, as it came to be termed, Moore, Ford, and the department managers met to assess where they were.

"The numbers work for now," Ford reported. "Still, there's no margin for error. Orders are as low as they have ever been, but they're stable. I think we've hit bottom. If we can maintain current workforce costs and productivity, we can survive, assuming the economy comes back in the next twelve to eighteen months."

Moore turned to the department managers. "Can you hang in?"

Charte grimaced. "I'm not sure, Owen." She handed Moore and Ford folders. "I've done two studies. The first shows labor per unit, expressed in both employee hours and dollars, before and after the implementation of the Rescue Plan. The second shows the number of days it takes from receipt of an order until the date of shipment, again both before and after the Rescue Plan."

"What's the conclusion, Flo?"

"We're spending 25 percent less in employee hours and 30 percent less in dollars per unit, and we've only added two additional days to the usual sixteen-day order-to-shipment period."

"Spectacular. What's the issue?"

"I'm pushing my people past their limits, and I'm not sure they can keep it up. They come in early and stay late to get their work done and are afraid that if they ask for overtime, they'll be the next to go. I'm not sure all of them will be willing stay here under these conditions. There's a lot, and I mean a *lot,* of grumbling. If I lose even one experienced employee in a key slot for any length of time, I'm afraid the house of cards will collapse."

"Noah, can we add a body or two to Production?"

Ford shook his head. "No, not now. We need three more months of stability. Then we can go to the bank and probably extend our line of credit. However, if we show even the slightest inability to stay this course, we're cooked."

"Flo?"

"I guess there's not much I can do, is there? I'll beg and plead. I'll use unpaid interns, illegal immigrants, and my eight-year-old."

"You're the best, Flo. Let them know that if they put in the extra time and effort now, I won't forget. They'll be taken care of once we get through this." Moore turned to the others. "Anybody else?"

Both Administration and Design reported that they were stable, but morale was suffering. Before the Rescue Plan, everyone seemed upbeat, and there was a sense of cooperation with management. Now, they reported, the employees were stone-faced and, in some cases, borderline hostile. Price, the department manager for Sales and Marketing, was especially troubled.

"Something is going on, Owen. My salespeople hardly speak to me. I see them meeting in groups without me. That never happened before. I'm seeing similar things when I walk through the offices and the production area. It's not the same place."

"Of course, it's not, Lois. Of course, they're unhappy. They'd have to be. I'll make myself more visible and try to help out in the morale area. Here's the point, though. I hate to put it in these terms, but do they really have a choice? Nobody's hiring. Everyone's laying off people. Where are they going to go? They're stuck here, *and they know it*. There's a morbid upside to this economy. *They've got no alternatives*. You've got to keep pushing them. Don't worry. They're not going anywhere."

Bruce Easley held the chief assembler job for eight years. It was a crucial position: he coordinated the assembly of the component parts into the finished product. Charte noticed that the production numbers had fallen off, and identified Easley as the bottleneck. Approximately once every half hour, Easley had to lift components off the production line and carry them to an adjacent assembly area. It was obvious to Charte that he could not do it at his usual pace—he would try, grimace, put the components down, and hold his shoulder. Easley was a slight, delicate man, but a hard worker who was liked and respected by his co-workers. The conveyor operator periodically slowed the line until Easley could catch up.

Charte knew that she could not afford to lose Easley, and at the same time, she could not afford to have Easley slow the line. Following Moore's lead, she decided to give Easley a not-so-subtle message during one of her routine walk-throughs.

"Hey, Bruce, how's things?"

"Same old, Flo. How're you doing?"

"Crummy, to be honest. Our production numbers are being looked at every day through a magnifying glass. Owen and Noah keep telling me that there are tons of people out there looking for jobs, and I should replace anybody who can't do what we need to do around here. It's not good."

"That's really heartwarming."

"Hey, they're under a lot of pressure, too. The economy. Maybe you've heard about it?"

Easley remained expressionless.

"So look, Bruce. Our numbers haven't been great the last week or so. Unless things turn around, I have to start looking for the problem. Keep your eyes open for me and let me know what's causing the slowdown? If I've got to fire somebody, I want to make sure it's the right somebody, OK?"

"No problem, Flo."

Diane Fast, a sales representative, walked sheepishly into Lois Price's office. Fast was a dedicated and productive employee who had successfully managed a key territory for many years. But she had her baggage—Price thought she was an irrational health nut. If the hormones used to grow the meat in the local burger joint didn't give her cancer, the exhaust emissions she ingested on the ride over would. Fast ate only certified organic foods, drank no alcohol, exercised religiously, and bought into every fad health craze she could find. It was always something, but still, her productivity advantages had always outweighed her quirks.

"Lois, can I speak with you?"

"Sure. Have a seat."

"Lois, I hate to do this. But life's too short as it is." Fast started to cry.

"Diane, what? Tell me."

"Lois, I've decided to have some surgery. It'll happen in three weeks. I'll be out about six weeks."

"If you don't mind telling me, what kind of surgery?"

"I'm having a double mastectomy."

Price was dumbstruck. Fast, the health fanatic, of all people. "Diane, I'm so sorry. When were you diagnosed?"

"There is no diagnosis. I'm doing this as a preventive measure."

Price had heard of women with serious and undeniable family histories of breast cancer that chose this course. "Wow. So, there's a history of breast cancer in your family?"

"No, but it doesn't matter. I've been doing a lot of reading. Many authorities feel that much of breast cancer is caused by environmental factors we can't escape. Family history and genetics have nothing to do with it. There's nothing wrong with me now. But I'm not taking any chances."

Price was, again, dumbstruck. "Diane, look . . ." Fast interrupted, angry.

"I know you think this is silly, Lois. But I'm entitled to my opinion. I want to be there as my grandchildren grow up. It's my body. It's my decision. I'm only here to give you the courtesy of advance notice, not to seek your approval."

"OK, Diane. Enough said. I don't mean to intrude."

"Thank you, Lois." Fast got up and turned toward the door.

"Diane, wait. We've known each other a long time. I think you'd agree that the company has treated you well. I need a favor."

"What is it, Lois?"

"I have to ask you not to do this now. You know the situation. Give me at least three months. Please."

"Lois, I can't do that. I need to fully recover before my sons come home from college. I want to spend the summer being able to do things with my family. If I don't have the surgery now, I won't be able to get it done for almost a year, and I'm not taking the risk. Plus, it will be hanging over my head. I'm geared up for it. It's scheduled. I need to get it over with."

"Will a few months really matter? You look fine. Better than I do, for sure."

Fast started to cry. "This is my life, not yours, Lois. Let me do what I have to do."

Price tried, without a lot of success, to conceal her anger. Moore Company's survival and Price's livelihood were being imperiled by a woman who, in Price's view, refused to listen to reason. "I can't stop you, Diane. But I can't guarantee that your job will be here when you get back. I'll do my best, but it'll be up to Owen. We'll probably fill your job, and maybe we can work you in later. No guarantees, though."

"You'd really do that to me? I've given this company all I have. That stinks, Lois."

"I know it does, Diane. Call the jerks in Washington and on Wall Street who put us in this financial mess."


Moore's intercom beeped. "Owen, it's Noah. Can I stop by? I need to discuss something."

"Sure. Now's fine."

Ford walked in. He looked shaken.

"Owen, my son's coming home."

Ford's son, a U.S. Army Ranger, had been deployed in Afghanistan. Moore shook Ford's hand. "That's great! When's the party?"

"He's been hurt, Owen. We're told he's going to be OK, but he was wounded pretty badly. We're setting up a bed in our family room. There will be a nurse there, 24/7. I need to be there, too. He needs family. I need to focus on him for the next couple of months or so."

Moore took a deep breath, and measured his words. "Noah, please. I need you here every day—you'll have nights and every weekend to spend with him. Maybe we can do a couple half-days a week instead?"

"Owen, he's my son. He's been hurt." Ford took a deep breath, trying to gather himself. "This is a time in his life and my life when my being there will really make a difference."

Moore stopped himself. He had been thinking for some time that most of what Ford did could be outsourced at a much lower cost, but Ford had been a loyal employee for many years, and Moore had never been able to pull the trigger. Moore now realized that Ford was opening a door that Moore had not been able to open himself.

"OK, Noah. You do what you need to do. We'll talk about it later."

Three weeks later, Moore called Ford. After the niceties, Moore said what he had to say. "Noah, things aren't getting much better, and I really need a full-time CFO to help me make decisions. I had our CPA firm assign an accountant three days a week and that seems to be doing the trick—at a lot less money. I'm not sure what we'll do when you're ready to come back. We can talk about it then, OK?"

"Sure we can, Owen. Sure." Ford hung up. It was the last time Ford and Moore spoke to each other.

Moore's secretary had, as usual, stacked the mail on his desk. On top was a registered letter. The return address was engraved on the back of the envelope: "Susan Fairley, Esquire." Moore had that feeling in his stomach again, the one he had on the witness stand during the Goode Manufacturing trial. He closed his office door, opened the envelope, and read the letter.

> Dear Mr. Moore:
>
> I have been retained to represent twelve former employees and eight current employees of Moore Company.
>
> After a lengthy and detailed investigation, I have concluded that Moore Company has perpetrated a series of unlawful actions directed toward its workforce. By way of example, these actions include violations of the Family Medical

and Leave Act, the Americans with Disabilities Act, the Pregnancy Discrimination Act, and the Fair Labor Standards Act. In addition, my investigation has revealed unlawful discrimination based on age, gender, and religion, along with instances of unlawful retaliation, breach of contract, and numerous other violations of employee rights.

I am willing to discuss a prompt and fair resolution of these issues. Such a resolution will necessarily require compensation to my clients for all economic losses suffered in the past and on an ongoing basis into the future; compensation for emotional distress damages; payment of all counsel fees and expenses; reinstatement of terminated employees; and other damages to be discussed.

If a settlement is not concluded, I plan to seek punitive damages to the extent the law permits—given the breadth of the assault on employee rights you have perpetrated, it will not be difficult to prove your willful and reckless conduct. To the extent the law permits, I will also seek to obtain a judgment against you in your individual capacity.

I have already filed charges with the Department of Labor and the Equal Employment Opportunity Commission in order to garner their assistance in my ongoing investigation.

I suggest you have your counsel notify me immediately with respect to your intentions. Failing to hear from you within one week of the date of your receipt hereof, I will proceed without further notice.

Moore shuffled through the rest of his incoming mail, and saw letters from the DOL and the EEOC. He dialed the number of his attorney, Louis D. Case. It struck him as a bad sign that he knew it by heart.

"I want you to throw this back into Fairley's face, Lou. I've had it. I can absolutely prove that I *had* to lay off employees. The company was running out of money. I had no other options."

"You're entitled to lay off employees, Owen. That's not the issue. The issue is *whom* you let go and how you ran the business after the layoffs."

"Come on, Lou. It's my butt on the line. I'm the one who put all I had into this company. I'm the one who guaranteed the bank debt. Are you telling me that some lawyer who doesn't know the first thing about this business gets to tell me who works here and how I run things? Does she also get to tell me whom I buy my materials from, how much I pay, whom I sell to, and what price I charge? Does she pay the bank if I can't? This is getting silly, Lou."

"Calm down. Think of it this way. You get to decide who works there, but at the same time, you can't fire people just because of their race. You buy that, right?"

"So what's the point?"

"The point is that your rights aren't absolute, Owen. There are limits and exceptions."

"I get that. I have the right of free speech, but I can't yell 'fire' in a crowded theater. Freedoms aren't absolute. We all give up some freedoms for the greater good . . . Yadayadayada. I understand the concept of a civilized society."

"Sometimes that concept produces laws you might disagree with, Owen. One man's civilized society can be another man's arbitrary dictatorship."

"All very interesting, Lou. But, again, what's the point? We focused purely on productivity, just like you're supposed to do in a business. Those who were most likely to produce stayed. Those who were the least likely to produce went. I didn't discriminate. I judged everyone by the same standard. I kept the people who could do the best job, and I insisted that they work as hard as they could. Are you telling me *that's* against the law?"

"Sometimes it can be. That's exactly what I'm telling you."

Moore had reached his limit. "This is crazy. I'm a commonsense kind of guy and you're telling me to throw out my common sense. I feel like Alice in Wonderland. Up is down and down is up. Right is wrong and wrong is right. Am I also supposed to buy high and sell low?"

Case understood Moore's frustration and knew it was better to let him vent. "OK, Lou. So, I'm at the mercy of a legal system that makes no sense to me. Things could be worse. What do I do?"

"I've got a list of Fairley's clients. I need the facts on each one—what was done, and why. I'd like you to tell your department managers and everyone in upper management that I'm going to be doing an investigation, and they need to give me all, and I mean *all*, the information and documents I ask for. I need to know what Fairley knows, and what she'll be able to find out if this ever becomes a lawsuit. In the meantime, I'll tell Fairley that I'm investigating the allegations and will contact her when we're done."

"You know, Lou, I'm all for employee rights. But I always thought that Job One was making sure there was a company that keeps the employees employed. How can doing what's necessary to stay in business be illegal?"

"I'm not a philosopher, Owen. My job is to stop the analysis at 'what is' and leave the question of 'what should be' to others. At least for now, I suggest you do the same. Whether you or I agree with it, the law is still the law, and we have to deal with it. Once I get the facts, I'll be able to reach some conclusions and report back."

"You'll 'report back.' Wonderful. That's lawyer-speak for, 'Give me a week, and I'll tell you all the crimes you never knew you committed.'"

"I can probably get you into one of those minimum-security places with the tennis courts, Owen. Your game could use some work."

"Seriously, Lou, I have foreign competitors who don't have to deal with this stuff. We can't compete if we're constantly walking on eggshells, not knowing when the government's going to come out of thin air and give us another reason why we can't do what makes business sense."

"Let me do my job, Owen. Then we'll talk."

Even as he was saying it, Case knew that by the time he completed his investigation, he'd be giving Moore a hefty dose of bad news.

■　■　■

## The Employment Law Flyover: A Little Knowledge Is Not Necessarily a Dangerous Thing

As the saying goes, "A little knowledge can be a dangerous thing." The saying is true enough, but only to a point—a little knowledge *can* be dangerous *if* you think you know more than you really do, and *if* you don't understand how to use the knowledge you have. But having *no* knowledge or the *wrong* knowledge can be *much* more dangerous. Owen Moore and his management team will learn that lesson the hard way.

Consider, again, the car-ownership analogy. Most people are not car experts, but they have just enough car knowledge to stay out of trouble. They have a general sense for how the engine is supposed to sound, how the car is supposed to handle, what the warning lights mean, how to check their tire pressure, when they're supposed to take the car in for regular maintenance, and so on. When they see or hear something unusual, and when the car is due for service, they take it to someone who knows what they're doing. The little knowledge they have is anything but dangerous—on the contrary, it maximizes return on investment and minimizes disasters.

The people who prove the wisdom of the old saying are the people who overestimate their knowledge. It's a character flaw, *not* a knowledge flaw: They refuse to recognize their limitations. They assume, with false bravado, that they know how to fix the thump under the hood or the sudden drop in gas mileage, and they dive in with predictable results. Yet it doesn't have to be that way—with some coaching and learned wisdom, they can find the line between what they know and what they don't know, use the former, and find help with respect to the latter.

Then there are the people who see no need for even a little knowledge. They walk blindly through minefields without the information required either to avoid problems or to recognize and fix them when they arise. They are the ones who don't know or care enough to change their oil or pay attention to the "check engine" light. You can usually find them stuck on the side of the road, waiting for a tow truck.

This same logic applies, in spades, to the intersection between law and business—and most especially to the counterintuitive, sometimes unimaginable, employee vs. employer collisions that so often occur at that intersection. You don't have to be a mechanic to prevent most forms of car trouble, and you don't have to be a lawyer to keep your business out of most forms of legal trouble. All you need is the will to obtain a little knowledge in the right categories, combined with just enough insight so you know when to use it, how to use it, and when to stop short and bring in the experts.

This section provides the modicum of knowledge you'll need to function in the employee vs. employer world. It is not a course in employment law; it couldn't be, and it doesn't have to be. Think of this section as an employment law flyover from about thirty thousand feet up, focusing on the 10 percent of employment law that covers 90 percent of the problems most businesses will face.

Once you have seen and understood the pertinent employment law landscape from this perspective, the "How was I supposed to know *that*?" question will become less troublesome. You'll still only see the tips of the most significant icebergs, but you'll recognize them for the hazards they present, and you'll understand the logic underlying the evasive maneuvers you'll have to use to avoid disaster. You'll continue to have lots of questions, but they'll be the *right* questions. The Attorney Hotline relationship mentioned in Chapter One will become a hugely important and beneficial resource.

■ ■ ■

IN MANY WAYS, THE EMPLOYMENT LAW flyover on which we are about to embark is a reverse travelogue—a tour of the places you do *not* want to go. It is predicated on the simple truth that you cannot avoid a problem unless you know it's out there.

The employment law flyover begins with the "employee at-will" and related doctrines, and the exceptions that have swallowed the rule. You might think you have the right (and, indeed, the obligation) to hire, fire, and manage your employees in a way that maximizes profits. You do not. The flyover will continue into the areas that define how the law requires companies, and those who work for companies, to treat their employees. There are some important things you're allowed and not allowed to do in the workplace—and, often, it's tough to tell the difference. When we're done, we'll be ready to begin the process of exploring the solutions to the problems the flyover will reveal.

⇢ **You might think you have the right (and, indeed, the obligation) to hire, fire, and manage your employees in a way that maximizes profits. You do not.**

## Can I Fire At-Will?

Owen Moore and his management team believed what most employers believe. It's a free country with a free enterprise system. We have the right to use our judgment, our instincts, to hire whom we want, fire whom we want, promote whom we want, and manage the business the way we want. If we do it well, we win; if we do it wrong, we lose—simple as that. Sure, there are certain obvious and well-known restrictions, such as unlawful racial discrimination, overtime requirements, minimum wage standards, safety regulations, things like that. But one thing is *certainly* clear: *we can keep and promote the employees who are more productive and get rid of or demote the employees who are less productive.*

In fact, that *is* the general rule. Most jurisdictions in the United States subscribe, more or less, to the "employee at-will" doctrine: unless there's an agreement that says otherwise, employees are classified as "at-will," meaning the employer can terminate them, or they can leave—at any time, for good reasons, bad reasons, or no reasons. The logical corollary to the employee at-will rule is that while at-will employees remain employed, the employer can promote them, discipline them, and generally manage them as the employer sees fit. Importantly, the reasoning and justification for the employer's decisions do not have to be well founded or even rational. The boss has a gut feeling that a particular employee is bad for morale and fires him. The boss enjoys working with one employee and promotes him even though he is less qualified than another, less likable employee. In most jurisdictions, that's the boss's prerogative.

However, this is one of those general rules that can be understood only through the study of its exceptions. The rule is peppered with so many holes, conditions, and quirks that it has lost all meaning and authority.

Alright, you're thinking, so I just look up the list of exceptions, and go from there. Not quite. As will be seen, figuring out what the exceptions mean, how courts have interpreted them, and the boatloads of exceptions to the exceptions is itself a course of study.

On top of that, employment law is not only voluminous and oblique, it's layered. Like many other bodies of law that affect businesses, it is an amalgam of federal laws that sit on top of state laws that sit on top of local laws. Federal law, in the form of congressional legislation, executive orders, and regulations promulgated by federal agencies, reigns mainly supreme. It embodies a host of largely unforeseeable "How was I supposed to know *that*?" exceptions to the employee at-will general rule. States and localities are not permitted to enact laws that diminish the effect of federal laws, but they *can* add laws of their own that make existing federal laws even more restrictive. Frequently, they do so.

For instance, Congress has established certain criteria that cannot be considered when making employment decisions, such as an employee's race, nationality, or gender. States and localities cannot eliminate any of the criteria on the federal list, but they can add their own, additional criteria—such as sexual orientation, workers' compensation history, sickle-cell traits, unfavorable military discharge, political affiliation . . . and so on. Some federal laws only apply to employers with fifty employees. Many states and localities have lowered the qualifying number to twenty-five or even fewer employees. Some states have even done away with the at-will rule itself, and mandated that employee terminations must be justifiably based on qualifications or performance, not on the employer's personal preferences for certain employee traits over others. What's legal in Pennsylvania might be illegal in California, and what's legal in Cincinnati might be illegal in New York City. And courts in one state might interpret the same legal language differently than courts in another state.

Here's the point. Employers need to know that the employee at-will rule is a rule in name only. The real world of employee-employer relations presents a vastly different set of do's and don'ts. In order to function in that real world, employers need to understand the primary categories into which the exceptions to the employee at-will rule reside, so they'll know them when they see them.

**The Americans with Disabilities Act**

The Americans with Disabilities Act, known as the ADA, might be the most misconstrued and least understood of the federal exceptions to the employee at-will concept. The act applies to private employers with fifteen or more employees (though many states have reduced that threshold). The ADA was originally enacted in 1990. Over the years, lawsuits were filed seeking interpretations of its precise meaning and scope, and ultimately, the Supreme Court issued a series of business-friendly rulings that restrictively defined some of the ADA's key terms in ways that generally favored employers. In response, Congress passed the ADA Amendments Act (ADAAA), which became effective in January 2009.

Here's what the ADA mandates, as amended by the ADAAA (with the key statutory terms italicized): the ADA prohibits employers from discriminating against *qualified* applicants and employees with a *disability*, and it requires employers to provide *reasonable accommodations* as needed to enable disabled applicants and employees to perform their job. The financial consequences for violations can be monumental.

The ADA sounds reasonable and laudable. If an applicant or an employee is qualified, there is no justification for discriminating against him merely because he has a disability. In addition, if a disabled person needs a reasonable break here and there to help him do his job, big deal. That's not much to expect from the business community in a country that prides itself on its inclusiveness and respect for the individual.

···> **The Americans with Disabilities Act, known as the ADA, might be the most misconstrued and least understood of the federal exceptions to the employee at-will concept.**

Rewind to Florence Charte. Forced to impose layoffs due to dire financial pressures, Charte focused on two employees with physical conditions that prevented them from doing all facets of their jobs. One employee had a bad knee that kept him from climbing stairs, which he had to do once or twice a day. Another spent the vast majority of his day as a dispatcher but was required to fill in on the loading dock once in a while and claimed that he couldn't lift more than ten pounds. Other employees had to step in and do what these employees could not do, limiting the efficiency of Charte's department and making them the most logical candidates for layoff.

Could Charte's decision possibly violate the ADA?

The ADA only applies to employees who have a "disability." In order for the ADA to apply, therefore, these employees would have to be "disabled." The most that can be said about them is that one has a bum knee that restricts stair climbing but little else, and the other, like many people, can't lift anything too heavy. Does that make them disabled?

The ADA, together with the ADAAA, says that an individual is disabled if he is "substantially limited" in "a major life activity." In the ADAAA, countermanding a run of restrictive court decisions, Congress directed that the term *substantially limited* be liberally and broadly construed. Congress similarly expanded the definition of *a major life activity*. In addition to the fundamentals, such as seeing, hearing, walking, and so on, *a major life activity* now encompasses, for instance, caring for oneself, performing manual tasks, eating, sleeping, standing, lifting, bending, learning, reading, concentrating, thinking, communicating . . . and much more. The definition also includes malfunctions in a variety of bodily functions, such as the immune system, the digestive system, neurological functions, reproductive functions, and a range of psychological disorders—think diabetes, colitis, infertility, depression, dyslexia . . .

Here's the takeaway: *disabled* does not mean what you probably think it means. In the ADA context, an individual does not have to be incapacitated, or anything close to it, to be disabled.

There's more: Suppose an applicant for a sales position has a facial scar or some other cosmetic disfigurement you think might be off-putting to potential customers. According to the ADA, cosmetic disfigurements can be disabilities.

How about this . . . An employee has a heart condition that would otherwise be disabling, but he's taking a medication and has no symptoms or problems. Or, an employee has a hearing loss, but with a hearing aid, he can hear almost normally. Or, he has diabetes that is well controlled by insulin. Or, he is HIV positive, but is stabilized by medication and has no apparent symptoms. The Supreme Court had ruled that those individuals are not disabled within the meaning of the ADA because, thanks to available treatments, they are fully functional. The ADAAA reversed that. Now, an employer must ignore these kinds of curative and mitigating measures, and look only at the underlying untreated impairment to determine if an employee is disabled. An individual who has a fully controlled medical condition can still be disabled.

Alcoholism? It's a protected disability (though that doesn't mean an employee can drink on the job). Former illegal-drug user? Again, it's a protected disability so long as the employee is not a current user.

OK, so be it. But as noted previously, a disabled applicant or employee still has to be *qualified* for the job—the ADA says you cannot discriminate against a *qualified* disabled person based on his disability. The employees Charte selected for layoff were *not* qualified—one couldn't make it up the stairs, and the other couldn't lift more than ten pounds.

The ADA, however, defines a qualified employee as one who can perform the "essential functions" of his job—not *all* the functions, just the *essential* functions. Climbing stairs and lifting boxes were only minor parts of the workday for the employees Charte had fingered for layoff. A court would probably find that even though they couldn't handle these tangential duties, they could handle the *essential* functions of their jobs.

Plus, the ADA requires an employer to provide a disabled employee with a "reasonable accommodation" if that's what it takes for him to be able to fulfill the essential functions of his job. A reasonable accommodation could easily include having another employee provide a minor amount of intermittent help—such as, in the case of Moore's employees, carrying something up stairs or lifting a twenty-pound box.

Remember how Charte treated Bruce Easley? Normally, an employer only has to provide a reasonable accommodation if an employee asks for it, but Charte purposefully intimidated Easley into keeping his mouth shut—and that's going to cause formidable problems for Moore Company.

Suppose you've got two applicants for a job, or you have to choose which of two employees will be laid off. One needs a $2,000 special telephone, or a $3,000 set of crane controls, or a $1,000 office chair, or an extra half-hour break in the middle of the day to take medication—and if he gets that extra help, he can perform the essential functions of his job just fine. The other needs no special help of any kind. You *cannot* make your choice based on who is going to cost you more; that would constitute discrimination based on disability.

If you are dealing with a disabled applicant or employee who lets you know that he needs some help to do the job, you *must* enter into a dialogue with the applicant or employee for the purposes of determining what sort of reasonable accommodation would do the trick. How far do you have to go in order to be "reasonable"? You don't have to change the nature of the job, and you don't have to break the bank, but you will have to talk with the employee about what might work, and so long as the accommodation does not cause the employer to suffer an undue hardship, it's a reasonable accommodation in the eyes of the ADA.

Remember when Charte decided to lay off an employee based on his medical history? The employee had been out on medical leave in the past, but was now just fine—no apparent disability of any kind remained. Charte, however, figured that the employee might be an absenteeism risk in the future, and that he therefore made a logical layoff candidate.

The ADA outlaws that as well—being "regarded as" having a disability because of, for example, a past condition is itself a protected disability under the ADA, and an employer cannot discriminate against an employee on that basis. So, for instance, if an employee has had a heart attack or cancer and has fully recovered, an employer cannot treat that employee as if he is or might become disabled.

The ADA can be burdensome, for sure. So it would make sense to weed out potentially disabled individuals from the applicant or employee pool before they become an expensive problem. With respect to applicants, however, the ADA prohibits an employer from asking questions about potential disabilities or medical conditions at any time before a job offer is made. The only permitted areas of inquiry are those that seek information about the applicant's background and qualifications for the position—can he do the essential functions of the job? If the applicant has an apparent disability, the employer can ask if the applicant will require a reasonable accommodation. That's it.

After an applicant is offered a job, an employer can make disability-related inquiries *only if* you make the same inquiries of everyone in the same job category. For example, if all new factory employees have to have a physical, fine; if you single out only those you think may have a physical or mental issue, you've violated the ADA. If you discover that a prospective employee may have a disability, you cannot withdraw the offer of employment so long as the employee can perform the *essential* functions (remember, not necessarily *all* the functions) of the job with (or without) a reasonable accommodation.

As for existing employees, you can seek medical information only in accordance with tightly circumscribed limitations: you must have a reasonable belief, based on real, objective evidence, that an employee's ability to perform the essential functions of his job is impaired. Flo Charte's observations of Bruce Easley would likely qualify. But there are copious restrictions on what you can seek, how you can seek it, and what you can do with the information you obtain.

There's a lot more to the ADA. A *lot* more. And it's not all bad news for employers. There are limits to what an employer is required to do, and employees have certain responsibilities as well. Your job is to know enough about the ADA so you can spot potential problems *before* it's too late to do something about them.

## The Family and Medical Leave Act

I train a lot of executives and managers on employment law compliance issues. I'll often ask a group how they would respond if an employee asked for two months of unpaid leave during a time when it would be difficult for their company to let the particular employee go—maybe they are short staffed, maybe they're up against a deadline, maybe it's their busy season, whatever.

Most say that except for major health issues or true crises, they'd be unlikely to grant the leave, but they'd give the employee an opportunity to explain the reason. I tell them the employee's mother has diabetes and a heart condition, she's being treated in the hospital, she's not in any immediate danger but no one can predict the future, and the employee simply wants to be with her.

No way, not during a crunch, no more than a half day here or there unless there is a real emergency, many will say. Maybe a week, others will say, then let's see what's going on at work and with her condition. I'd give some time off, others say, but I'd want to know if there's a husband or other siblings who could pitch in before I decide how far to go.

Would it be reasonable, I ask them, if you told the employee that you were willing to compromise—he could take a week off without pay, but unless the situation really deteriorates, he's got to come back for at least a few days, or even a few half days, to help cover work emergencies, and then you'll decide where to go from there? They usually agree that's more than reasonable.

Now suppose, I tell them, that the employee says he's not going along with that no matter what you say and, instead, he says he's taking off the full two months unless his mother makes some kind of miraculous recovery. He's not going along with any compromises, and he's doing what he thinks is best. Period. What then?

Many say they would fire the employee on the spot for insubordination and for being unreasonable. Others say they'd keep their options open—he's going to leave no matter what, no sense making a scene, deal with it later, depends on how valuable the employee is. Some say they'd call HR or their lawyer.

I tell them to assume that the employee's absence will make it difficult to do what needs to be done for an important customer. What then? If he's not back in a week, I would hire a replacement, most of them say.

Finally, I ask those who have not already decided to fire the employee what they would do when the employee returns from leave. I'd try to find a spot for him, they usually say, but you can't make guarantees—you've also got to be fair to the replacement you hired. You do the best you can.

The next hour is spent discussing the numerous and serious violations of the Family and Medical Leave Act they all just committed, and how much it will probably cost to get out of the lawsuit.

The Family and Medical Leave Act (FMLA) was enacted in 1993 to provide a modicum of job security to employees who require time off from work because of their own serious health condition or to care for family members with serious health conditions or to care for newborn infants. It was Congress's stated goal to balance the needs of employees and their families against the legitimate interests of their employers, and Congress chose to do so by mandating that employers provide employees with unpaid leaves of absence coupled with guaranteed reinstatement, in limited, closely defined circumstances. The FMLA applies to employers with fifty or more employees—but be careful. Many states have reduced that threshold, and many more, as well as Congress itself, are seriously considering doing the same.

Like the ADA, the FMLA's stated goal is, on its face, legitimate and justifiable. As so often occurs, however, problems arise when that goal is translated into a mandated business reality, coupled with severe damage awards for violations. These problems seem to arise mainly in two contexts. First, many executives and managers still don't "get" the FMLA—the concept of being forced to grant lengthy unpaid leaves, especially in the face of screaming business exigencies, makes no sense to them, and they let their "get the job done" instincts take over. Second, even when executives and managers try in good faith to implement the FMLA, they can't figure out what it means—it has become a voluminous, esoteric, *extremely* detailed, and technical body of rules, regulations, and judicial opinions.

The first problem is simply solved: the law's the law; complain to your senator and congressional representative if you wish, but in the meantime, get over it.

The second problem is more difficult but also solvable. Remember the car analogy. You don't have to become an FMLA expert in order to deal with the FMLA. Most of the technicalities can and should be left to the lawyers and the HR professionals. They can design and implement practical preventive forms and procedures that tell you how to deal with most of the situations you will face when dealing directly with employees. All you need is a little FMLA knowledge— the kind of information that will help you avoid the traps your common sense might lead you into, the kind of information that will help you spot a nascent FMLA issue before it gets out of hand and, perhaps most important, the kind of information that will signal when it's time to bring in the experts.

Here are the basics of what you need to know:

*Who is eligible for how much FMLA leave?* Under the FMLA, an "eligible" employee may take up to twelve workweeks of unpaid leave (consecutively or in intermittent, shorter periods) during any twelve-month period, for any one of the following reasons:

**1.** To deal with the birth of a child and to care for the newborn child

**2.** To deal with adopting a child or accepting a child into foster care and to care for the child

**3.** To care for the employee's spouse, son, daughter, or parent with a "serious health condition"

**4.** Because a "serious health condition" makes the employee unable to perform one or more of the "essential functions" of his job

In 2009, the FMLA was amended to include another qualifying reason for leave: because of an employee's military service or to help relatives serving in the military. One aspect of the amendment provides up to twelve weeks annual unpaid leave to a spouse, parent, or child of a military service member to deal with the financial, travel, child care, and other logistical issues that military service might cause. Another aspect of the amendment provides up to twenty-six weeks annual unpaid leave to a spouse, parent, child, or "next of kin" to care for an injured military service member. (It's worth noting that there is another federal statute, the Uniformed Services Employment and Reemployment Rights Act [USERRA], that requires, subject to the usual array of technical conditions, *all* employers to rehire an employee who left for military service and then timely seeks to return to his job.)

*What's a "serious health condition"?* A key question is how "serious" does an employee's or an employee's family member's health condition have to be before it becomes a serious health condition entitling an employee to leave under the

FMLA? Basically, the FMLA defines *serious health condition* as any period of incapacity or treatment that requires an overnight stay in a medical facility or that requires more than three days of continuing treatment. Any period of incapacity due to pregnancy and prenatal care is also covered, as are incapacity from long-term conditions for which treatment is not effective (for instance, Alzheimer's, stroke, terminal diseases, etc.) and absences to receive treatments (and to recover from treatments) for serious health conditions (for instance, chemotherapy, physical therapy, dialysis, etc.).

Note that an FMLA serious health condition is not necessarily the same as an ADA disability. An ADA disability is generally an impairment that substantially limits one or more major life activities and not, for instance, an injury or condition that's temporary in nature. A broken leg or appendicitis that's on the mend is not a disability. A broken leg or appendicitis could be a serious health condition.

> ···> **All you need is a little FMLA knowledge—the kind of information that will help you avoid the traps your common sense might lead you into, the kind of information that will help you spot a nascent FMLA issue before it gets out of hand, and, perhaps most important, the kind of information that will signal when it's time to bring in the experts.**

*How can I make sure that an employee is telling me the truth?* Employers have the right to ask an employee who seeks FMLA leave to provide documentation from a health care provider certifying the existence of a serious health condition. This certification procedure is tightly defined and controlled—let the professionals, either your trained HR executive or outside counsel, handle it.

*Are all employees entitled to ask for FMLA leave?* Employees are eligible for FMLA leave if they (1) have been employed for at least twelve months, which need not be consecutive; (2) had at least 1,250 hours of service during the twelve-month period immediately before the leave started; and (3) are employed at a worksite at which the employer employs fifty or more employees within seventy-five miles (but, remember, some states have lessened these requirements).

*What about health insurance?* FMLA leave is unpaid, but an employer *must* maintain the employee's existing level of health coverage under a group plan while the employee is out on leave.

*What happens when the employee's leave is over?* This is monumentally important, and can cause huge practical problems. With very limited exceptions, at the end of FMLA leave, an employer *must* reinstate the employee into the same or an equivalent job as the one held when the leave began. An employer is entitled to request medical documentation pertaining to the employee's fitness to return.

*What if there is a dispute?* In the event of an FMLA-related disagreement, the most recent amendments to the FMLA require that employers and employees engage in a reasonable dialogue—*and that the content and results of the dialogue be documented.* Exactly what this means has not yet been fleshed out. But if nothing else, an employer should rethink any propensity to assert a "this is the way it is; take it or leave it" approach when it comes to FMLA issues. Talk, and take notes or otherwise document (for instance, through memos or e-mails) the efforts made to bridge any gaps. If, after a dialogue, the disagreement continues, and you are convinced you are right, so be it. But you must engage in and document the effort to reach an agreement—a good idea even if not mandated by the law.

*Anything else?* Yes, most definitely. There are mountains of other requirements that deal with an employer's obligation to notify employees about their rights, the records employers have to keep, an employee's obligation to notify an employer of the need for leave, how and when the leave is scheduled, whether an employee can be required to exhaust paid vacation and sick leave before taking FMLA leave, handling intermittent leave requirements, privacy issues, and so on and so on . . . and then some. In addition, remember that some states have changed the rules—even to the point of implementing mandatory paid leave programs. It's difficult to assimilate all the nuances and technicalities; that's why there are lawyers and HR professionals.

*What happens if I mess up?* The stakes are high. If you violate an employee's FMLA rights, you could be responsible for lost wages, lost employment benefits, the costs incurred by the employee while denied leave, interest, additional "liquidated damages" that could significantly increase the tab, reinstatement, attorneys' fees . . . you get the idea.

How does all of this play out in the real world? Think of it in this somewhat unpleasant (and just a bit overstated) way: the ADA and the FMLA force you to accommodate and spend money on employees who cannot or will not do their jobs. That's the primary reason why ADA and FMLA compliance comes so unnaturally to so many businesspeople—they run counter to primal business instincts.

Bruce Easley needs a lifting device that will cost you $3,000. If he doesn't get it, he'll slow down production to a point you can't afford. He's a good employee, but he's certainly not irreplaceable. Your concern for the bottom line tells you that maybe it's time to get someone who won't cost you money and who's got more of a future. The ADA imposes a different agenda.

Diane Fast wants to undergo surgery. You say she can take the time off, but please, it's no emergency, not now. She refuses. You can't believe that she won't work with you in a reasonable way. The FMLA says that if she undergoes surgery that fits the definition of "serious health condition," you owe her FMLA leave and reinstatement.

Noah Ford wants to care for his injured son. Understandable, but it makes no business sense for you to hold his job open while he's gone. The FMLA says you've probably got to do it anyway.

And so it goes with respect to the office manager who wants to take off twelve consecutive weeks after the adoption of a child, the applicant who needs

> ⇢ **The ADA and the FMLA force you to accommodate and spend money on employees who cannot or will not do their jobs. That's the primary reason why ADA and FMLA compliance comes so unnaturally to so many businesspeople—they run counter to primal business instincts.**

extended breaks because of the effects of his medication, the distribution foreman who used to spend 10 percent of his time making an occasional delivery but can no longer drive, the receptionist who suffered a hearing loss and now needs special telephone equipment . . .

Your reactions to these kinds of situations might depend on your financial strength, current business conditions, how much you value and respect an employee, how reasonable you think the request may be, and a host of other factors and influences. Those reactions need to be shelved. You now know enough about the ADA and the FMLA to see the "disability" and "unpaid leave" red flags that arise from these types of interplays between employees and those who manage them. You can do some of the initial screening. Is this really a disability? Is this applicant qualified, even with a reasonable accommodation? Is this a serious health condition? Has this employee been with us long enough? You know enough to know that there is lots you don't know, and you'll be able to discern when you need expert input before making a decision that could come back to haunt you.

In short, unlike Owen Moore and his minions, you need to stop, set aside your instincts and opinions, and force yourself to see the issues, react, and make decisions on the basis of *the law*.

## Unlawful Discrimination

*Discrimination* has, understandably, become a dirty word. But it is important to remember that as a general rule you *are* allowed to discriminate against an employee. All successful businesses, for instance, discriminate against bad employees and in favor of good employees—a substantial part of effective management is accurately assessing who should be retained and promoted and who shouldn't. Discrimination can be a necessary and positive force. That's a primary reason why the at-will employment rule allows employers to exercise their discriminatory discretion freely, based on anything from a performance analysis to a gut feel.

But there are, as there always are, boundaries. Those boundaries are defined by the fact that the law seeks to prevent (and, therefore, punishes) certain forms of discrimination against employees in certain protected classes and has carved out cavernous exceptions to the employee at-will doctrine in the process.

There are two primary forms of unlawful discrimination against the employees in these protected classes, known as "disparate impact" and "disparate treatment" discrimination.

*Disparate impact discrimination: no safety in numbers.* Disparate impact discrimination occurs when an otherwise neutral and lawful employment practice unintentionally and disproportionately affects the employees in a protected class. For example, mandated strength requirements have been found to disproportionately exclude women. Requiring a high school diploma or mandating a certain score on a written language test have been ruled to put certain protected minorities in certain geographic areas at a disadvantage. Once the disparate impact is documented, in order to avoid liability the employer must show that the practice is job-related. For instance, a strength requirement might be valid in a warehouse job but not in a clerical position. A diploma or the ability to pass a written language test might be job-related in a supervisory position, but not for a position involving mainly manual labor.

> ⇢ **The law seeks to prevent (and, therefore, punishes) certain forms of discrimination against employees in certain protected classes and has carved out cavernous exceptions to the employee at-will doctrine in the process.**

In the most dangerous cases, the proof that an employer's policies disparately impact one or more protected classes comes in the form of a statistical analysis—for example, a company's workforce is comprised of 40 percent women, but only 20 percent of the management positions are held by women; or the average annual salary in a company is $61,000, but the average salary for African Americans in that company is $52,000. The obvious question becomes, why?

The key to avoiding disparate impact cases is to make certain that your recruitment, hiring, promotion, layoff, and other employment-related procedures and criteria are based on the real, provable requirements of your workplace. Sounds easy, but some of the largest companies in the country have gotten it wrong and been hammered with huge verdicts for hiring and promotion policies that, statistically, exclude people in protected classes. You'll need professional assistance.

In addition, strive to eliminate as many subjective employee-assessment criteria as you can—a subjective criterion can be easily infected by the biases of those who apply them, and courts know it. Again, this sounds easier than it is. Case in point: *Dukes vs. Wal-Mart*, the largest civil rights class action in history, involving almost two million female Wal-Mart employees with, perhaps, a billion dollars at stake. The Wal-Mart employees claim that Wal-Mart institutionalized procedures that allowed its executives to make key decisions involving raises and promotions on a subjective basis, and that this, combined with a corporate culture that included gender stereotyping, resulted in lower pay and fewer management opportunities for women. Wal-Mart has its defenses, to be sure, and the case is yet to be decided—but if the Wal-Mart employees can prove their allegation that Wal-Mart management allowed subjective bias to influence the decision-making process, the verdict could be a record breaker.

*Disparate treatment discrimination: can courts be mind readers?* Disparate treatment discrimination, on the other hand, arises when an employer *intentionally* discriminates against an employee *because* the employee is a member of the protected class. When an employee in a protected class brings a disparate treatment claim, he is alleging that the employer was biased against employees in that class and, because of that bias, the employer treated the employee less favorably than it did others.

Disparate treatment cases are on a dramatic upswing; they plague the executives, managers, and supervisors who have to make day-to-day employment-related decisions whereby they choose one applicant or employee over another. All it takes is for a single person to make a single accusation: "You [refused to hire me, did not promote me, disciplined me, laid me off . . .] because I am [a minority, a woman, a member of a certain religion . . .]." The employee's claim will survive in court if there's just a bit of evidence that supports it, at which point the burden shifts to you to prove you were motivated to do what you did for the right reasons, not the wrong reasons.

And there's the rub . . . we are back to the ubiquitous "my word against your word" issue. You *know* you did what you did for lawful reasons, but how will you prove what was in your mind? The trial becomes an exercise in judicial mind reading, with predictably unreliable results. Judges and juries seize on snippets of evidence that are no more revealing than tea leaves. You forcefully testify that you are not racially biased, but then that innocent e-mail you forwarded with the ethnic slur surfaces, and now there's a reason for a judge or jury to believe that, perhaps, you harbor some racial bias after all. Lots of companies have swallowed the bitter pill of making employment decisions for the right reasons, only to have a judge or jury find that they made their decisions based on the wrong reasons.

More about that in the next section, when we discuss preventive and problem-solving techniques. For now, just keep in mind that disparate treatment discrimination cases play out on that stage. In the meantime, it's crucial to understand the protected classes—the primary categories in which the employee at-will rule takes a back seat, and in which you have to be especially careful.

*Race, color, sex, national origin, religion.* The core, federal anti-discrimination law is known as Title VII: it prohibits discrimination based on a person's race; color (for example, favoring light-skinned members over dark-skinned members of a race); sex (meaning "gender," including favoring either gender over the other or requiring conformance with male or female stereotypes); national origin (such as birthplace, ancestry, culture, native language, accent, a name associated with a particular ethnic group, attendance at or participating in groups or activities associated with a particular ethnic group, and so on); and religion. Title VII applies only to employers with at least fifteen employees, but many state and local laws reduce that threshold.

Title VII cases arise when an employee claims that he was discriminated against (that is, he was not hired, was laid off, did not receive training, was disciplined, was not given a promotion, and so on) based on membership in one of these protected classes. Sometimes, an employee will find smoking-gun evidence proving that his employer was motivated by, for instance, racial, religious, or gender bias—public statements of bias; an uncontroverted and lengthy history of, for instance, promoting Caucasians or men and refusing to promote minorities or women even though the latter were objectively more qualified than the former; and so on. More often, however, these cases usually unfold through circumstantial evidence. A female employee who was fired, for example, might introduce testimony documenting that the supervisor who fired her never gave her any warnings while similarly situated men were given chance after chance to overcome poor work performance. She might compare her qualifications and work product with those of men in similar jobs who were not fired. She might prove that her supervisor frequently ate lunch and joked around with the men but not with her. The employer will argue that whatever decisions were made were based on job performance, and might reference the testimony of co-workers or written job evaluations. Ultimately, a court decides whom to believe.

Religious discrimination cases have become especially dicey and difficult and are worth discussing in a bit more detail. The number of cases charging religious discrimination claims has skyrocketed, and some of that is doubtlessly associated with post-9/11 religious tensions. Religious harassment cases (another form of discrimination), dealt with later in this section, are also on the rise, evidencing the fact that the workplace is a cauldron in which people of different backgrounds who might not otherwise choose to interact are forced to do so.

Title VII makes clear that you cannot allow your hiring, firing, compensation, promotion, or other management decisions to be influenced by an individual's religion. It doesn't matter that you or your employees want to associate with people of the same religion. It doesn't matter that your customers would prefer to associate with people of the same religion.

However, what happens when—based on the practices of his religion—an applicant or employee insists on certain days off or special breaks for prayer or refuses to perform certain tasks associated with his job? Generally, an employer will be required to accommodate the religious needs of an applicant or employee *unless* doing so would cause the employer to incur more than token costs or more than merely minor inefficiencies or burdens on other employees. If an employer can, within those criteria, feasibly reschedule or rejigger work assignments, it will be required to do so—but, if not, the employer will be justified in refusing.

Applicants and employees who seek to dress in religious garb, wear religion-based hairstyles (for instance, dreadlocks), and so on often claim that employer dress codes constitute religious discrimination. An employer's bona fide health or safety concerns will generally prevail over an employee's or applicant's religious garb or hairstyle. If, however, an employer's objection is based only on image or customer-reaction concerns, the employee or applicant will likely prevail. It's a case-by-case analysis, one on which you'll need expert guidance.

A second problem starts with the legal definition of "religion" itself. Federal law defines "religion" broadly, to include moral or ethical beliefs as to what is right or wrong and which are sincerely held with the strength of traditional religious views. To be protected under federal law, a "religion" need not be based upon a divinity, and there need be no meeting place or congregation. All that is required is a broad-based, truly held belief system that guides one's life. It does not have to be traditional or even comprehensible. It can be a "religion" if the employee who claims to be guided by it is the only believer.

*Age discrimination.* A federal statute passed in 1967, the Age Discrimination in Employment Act (ADEA), added another protected class to the list—applicants and employees who are forty and older. You can, under federal law, refuse to hire or promote someone because he is too young. But, with respect to employees who are at least forty, your motivation cannot be based on your view that they're too old. Perhaps as a function of our aging population, the volume of age discrimination claims has been increasing in scary proportions.

The ADEA applies to employers with twenty or more employees but, again, remember that some states and localities have enacted their own age discrimination laws that lower this benchmark, as well as the "forty and older" threshold.

There is a complex array of exceptions based on, for instance, situations in which age is a real factor in terms of an individual's ability to do his job (airline pilots, police officers, etc.), mandatory retirement programs, seniority systems, and similar situations.

Flo Charte's goal to make her department younger and more energetic by terminating the older employees might have made business sense to her and Owen Moore, but under the ADEA, it was blatantly illegal.

*Pregnancy discrimination.* The Pregnancy Discrimination Act (PDA), passed in 1978, added another protected class. It outlaws discrimination based on pregnancy, childbirth, and related medical conditions in employment, health insurance plans, disability insurance plans, and sick leave plans. It applies to employers with fifteen or more employees—but, again, some states and localities have reduced those standards.

The PDA, like other employment discrimination laws, prohibits discriminatory treatment in hiring, firing, compensation, job assignment, promotion, layoff or recall, training . . . and all other aspects of the employment relationship. As Flo Charte and Owen Moore discussed, a company might increase its survival prospects in tough times if it eliminates pregnant employees who will take maternity leave—which is precisely what the PDA prohibits. In addition, their strategy of weeding women out of the workforce because they *might* become pregnant is equally unlawful.

If a woman is temporarily disabled by pregnancy, childbirth, or a related condition, an employer is required to treat her just as it would treat any other temporarily disabled employee. For instance, if an employer has a practice of providing temporarily disabled employees with a period of paid leave, modifying their job requirements, accruing vacation and bonus entitlements, whatever, the employer must apply the same rules to temporary disabilities arising from pregnancy, childbirth, and related conditions. If the employer provides health insurance, it must cover pregnancy and childbirth to the same extent as it covers other medical conditions.

Remember that discrimination is discrimination, even if you are discriminating for what you think to be all the right reasons. You cannot, for instance, require that a pregnant woman be excluded from certain jobs she is capable of performing because, given her condition, you think it would be best that she not perform those jobs. And you cannot require a pregnant woman to take leave, paid or unpaid, because you think it would be best for her—she is entitled to work for so long as she wishes and is able.

*Retaliation.* Here's another protected class: individuals who assert or help others to assert their legally protected workplace rights. You cannot retaliate against individuals who, for instance, bring a workplace-related claim, participate in someone else's effort to bring a workplace-related claim, or lawfully complain about an unlawful employment practice, such as discrimination, harassment, ADA or FMLA issues, and so on. Various states have added a wide range of additional retaliation prohibitions as well—for instance, many states prohibit retaliation against employees who seek or recover workers' compensation. The Sarbanes-Oxley Act also protects whistle-blowers at public companies.

Think of it this way: if an employee has the legal right to seek redress or complain about something, an employer is not permitted to punish the employee, even subtly or indirectly, for exercising that right or for assisting anyone else to exercise that right. It doesn't matter that the employee was wrong so long as he acted honestly and in good faith. The same rules do not apply to employees who complain about their supervisor's personality or the amount of work they have to do—employers are generally free to deal with them as they think best. However, once the employee's conduct involves a legally protected right, an employer needs to be careful.

> --> **Remember that discrimination is discrimination, even if you are discriminating for what you think to be all the right reasons. You cannot, for instance, require that a pregnant woman be excluded from certain jobs she is capable of performing because, given her condition, you think it would be best that she not perform those jobs.**

The practical problem is, as it so often is, one of proof. The classic situation is one in which an employee makes a workplace-related claim, and six months later is demoted or fails to get a promotion or a requested job assignment, or is selected for layoff. The employee claims that he was retaliated against for having brought a lawful claim. The employer claims it was all based on performance, qualifications, seniority, whatever. The employee's case will be permitted to move forward merely because of the apparent linkage between making the claim and suffering the harm. It will then be up to the employer to offer proof showing that the employee's claim had nothing to do with the decision. This is a drum that cannot be pounded too frequently—the employer will face, yet again, a "my word against your word" situation, and it better have what it needs to prove it was right, that it did not unlawfully retaliate, or it will likely be proven wrong.

Retaliation can take many forms. Obviously, firing or disciplining a "complainer" can be problematic (depending on what the employee was complaining about). Nevertheless, many employers find themselves on the wrong side of a retaliation suit even though retaliation was the furthest thing from their mind. For instance, a woman complains about her manager's attitudes toward women. In response, thinking he is handling things correctly, the president of the company transfers her to another office in which women are more readily promoted. If the transfer, for instance, takes her farther away from home or involves the kind of work she would prefer not to do, that's retaliation. The correct approach is to address the potential discrimination and not let it remain in place while removing the complaining employee.

Had Owen Moore asked him, Lou Case would have explained the risks in Flo Charte's decision to eliminate complainers from the workplace. Charte's strategy might make financial sense; it did not make legal sense.

*Discrimination against applicants or employees who favor unions.* Employers who wish to avoid unionization often do what makes common sense: find and fire the pro-union employees. Doing so might be the fastest path to *insure* unionization, rather than avoid it.

This is an *extremely* complicated area of law, replete with trip wires and landmines. You *will* need professional guidance in this realm, which is governed mainly by the National Labor Relations Act (NLRA), a host of other statutes, and a heap of court and National Labor Relations Board (NLRB) decisions. The rules are voluminous and knotty, but there is one guiding principle that must be kept in mind: *employees who wish to unionize are protected under federal law.*

Employers cannot, for instance, retaliate against an employee for promoting unionization or for complaining about an employer's actions as they pertain to union issues. Employers cannot, explicitly or implicitly, reward those who disfavor unionization or threaten those who favor unionization. Employers cannot question employees about their unionization sentiments or ask employees for information about how other employees feel about the issue. Employers cannot ban workplace discussions about union matters while permitting workplace discussions on other nonwork-related topics. If an employer allows its employees to use company

**⋯⋙ Employers cannot, explicitly or implicitly, reward those who disfavor unionization or threaten those who favor unionization.**

facilities (for instance, the lunchroom) to talk about nonwork matters outside of work hours, the employer will usually be required to allow employees to use it to talk about union issues. If employers do not generally ban the distribution of pamphlets or other written materials in the workplace (for instance, get-out-the-vote campaigns, information about social gatherings), employers cannot ban the distribution of union literature in the workplace. There is a host of standards governing when an employer can ban the presence of nonemployee union organizers from company premises.

These concepts are replete with exceptions and conditions. Do not even think about going this alone.

*State and local additions to the list.* As discussed previously, states and localities frequently add to the list of protected classes. Some of the most frequent additions include bans on discrimination against persons eighteen or older based on age, against persons with disabilities beyond those that fall within the ADA, and against persons with AIDS/HIV. Other additions include, for instance, discrimination based on marital status, sexual orientation, transgender status, age considerations of any type, genetic testing information, political activities or affiliations, arrest record, height, weight, status as a smoker or nonsmoker, military status or service, or prior injuries. It's important to make sure you know the rules not only on a federal level, but also in the state and locale where you conduct business. When in Rome . . . be careful.

## Unlawful Harassment

In addition to making certain that your management decisions are not (and cannot be proven to be) based on an employee's status as a member of a protected class, employers must also make certain that their employees are not subjected to harassment because of their status as a member of a protected class.

Unlawful harassment is a type of discrimination, though it's generally not thought of in that way—it is discrimination in the sense that employees are singled out for adverse treatment (in this case, harassment) because of their race, gender, religion, or other protected class status. If an employer allows an employee to be mistreated by management or fellow employees because, for example, the employee has a disability or is a woman, a minority, or a Muslim, the employer can be liable to the employee for the so-called hostile work environment that results.

A hostile work environment, as that term is used in employment discrimination cases, can be comprised of slurs, jokes, offensive remarks or insults, offensive e-mails, letters, or pictures, shunning, threats, ridicule, mockery . . . so long as, again, the harassing conduct is based on protected class status (as opposed to, for example, personality conflicts, political disagreements, neighborhood disputes . . .). In addition, the law will ignore petty slights or insults, discourtesy, and intermittent teasing. The offending conduct must be severe and pervasive—more than the sorts of unpleasantry that a reasonable person should be able to tolerate. Once that line (the location of which often depends on what court you are in) is crossed, a hostile work environment case often follows, and the damages can be substantial.

It is important to understand that an employee can bring a successful hostile work environment claim even if the workplace goings-on are not directed at the employee. For instance, picture a situation in which one African American works in a department of twenty Caucasians. The Caucasian employees and the company's management might treat the African American employee cordially. But jokes demeaning African Americans are consistently distributed via e-mail "blasts." Derogatory and demeaning comments about other African Americans are the norm in meetings. Some employees hang obvious pictures and signs in their cubicles and lockers that belittle or threaten African Americans. In most courtrooms, that will be sufficiently severe and pervasive to make out a hostile work environment case.

···> **A hostile work environment, as that term is used in employment discrimination cases, can be comprised of slurs, jokes, offensive remarks or insults, offensive e-mails, letters, or pictures, shunning, threats, ridicule, mockery . . . so long as, again, the harassing conduct is based on protected class status (as opposed to, for example, personality conflicts, political disagreements, neighborhood disputes . . .).**

Harassment based on race or minority status has always been prevalent—racism persists in society, and in the microcosm of the workplace. In the post-9/11 world, claims based on religion, ethnic background, and national origin have dramatically spiked—again, the workplace is often a reflection of society in general. Employers often minimize harassment of this nature, excusing it as "free speech" or rationalizing that their role is not to regulate opinions and relationships. Neither excuse works: employers have the legal obligation to address unlawful harassment in the workplace, and the failure to do so can become very expensive.

Sexual harassment is probably the most frequently asserted type of unlawful harassment claim. Because of the plethora of sexual harassment claims, and because sex-based hostile work environment cases have produced a framework that will likely form the basis on which all types of hostile work environment cases will be adjudicated, it's worth reviewing these kinds of claims in some detail.

One type of sexual harassment case, the so-called quid pro quo case, involves a situation in which a supervisor (usually a male) conditions an underling's (usually a female's) compensation, promotion, or other job benefit on the underling's submission to the supervisor's unwelcome sexual advances. There was a time when a company could attempt to evade liability for its supervisor's quid pro quo conduct through the "What more could I do?" defense. The company would argue that it had outlawed such conduct through its published workplace policy manual, that it did not know about the conduct while it was occurring, and that it took the appropriate action against the supervisor as soon as it found out.

Those days have passed. If a supervisor engages in this sort of quid pro quo conduct and it affects the underling's job in some way (for example, the employee is forced to submit in order to obtain a job-related benefit or suffers a job-related detriment because of a refusal to submit), the employer is liable for what its supervisor did. Period. No defenses. Big damages. The message is clear: employers must do what it takes to prevent this kind of quid pro quo conduct from happening. More about that in the next section.

The other type of sexual harassment is a form of hostile work environment harassment, having nothing to do with quid pro quo. It does not have to be (though it can be) based on sexual come-ons or similar conduct. It can also be nonsexual in nature, so long as it is based on the employee's gender—as when a woman is harassed because she holds what is perceived to be a man's job or when a man is harassed because he is believed to be or is a homosexual. Companies successfully used the "What more could I do?" defense in these cases as well, especially when the harassment was perpetrated by the victim's fellow employees. It's not reasonable to make us pay, went the argument, when we told the employees not to do this kind of thing, when we didn't know it was happening, and when we stopped it as soon as we knew about it. How can you hold us responsible for the unknown actions of rogue employees?

The Supreme Court answered this question in 1998 (and in subsequent clarifying cases), and in the process changed the fundamentals of the employee-employer relationship. The Supreme Court ruled that if, as a result of harassment, the employee suffers some "tangible employment action"—for example, the employee is forced to quit or cannot work efficiently and loses a raise or is intimidated into forgoing efforts to advance—the employer is liable. No excuses. No defenses. Write a check. End of story.

And even if the employee does not suffer a tangible employment action, said the Supreme Court, the employer will *still* be liable to the employee for the employee's emotional distress, counsel fees, and, in some cases, even more *unless* the employer can prove two things: First, the employer must prove that it used reasonable efforts to prevent the harassing conduct from happening in the first place. Simply outlawing harassment in a policy handbook and hoping everything works out for the best is *not* good enough. The employer must show that it took a real, activist approach.

What that means in practice is that the employer must prove that it provided *regular and competent training* to its supervisory personnel from top executives to working foremen. In the eyes of the law, an employer that fails to train its supervisory personnel in the legal and practical principles that govern the rights of its employees has not made a serious effort to protect the rights of its employees. In the wake of these decisions, several states have enacted statutes fining employers who fail to train their supervisory personnel; but even in states where such statutes have not been enacted, the risks associated with the failure to train are now intolerable. More about that later in this chapter.

⋯⋯⋗ **Simply outlawing harassment in a policy handbook and hoping everything works out for the best is *not* good enough. The employer must show that it took a real, activist approach.**

Second, the employer must also prove that the complaining employee failed to take advantage of any preventive or corrective opportunities provided by the employer.

What that means in practice is that the employer must have established and publicized an effective complaint and investigation procedure through which employees can realistically report and resolve hostile work environment problems. The employer might escape liability if it can show that the employee did not utilize the procedure; that if the employee had done so, the employer would have thoroughly and objectively investigated; and that having done so, the employer would have solved any unlawful harassment problem before it got out of hand. More about that, too, later in this chapter.

The drift of the law seems to be signaling that this same analytical framework will be applied beyond the gender-based harassment context and utilized in all unlawful harassment cases—whether the harassment arises from an employee's disability, race, religion, or any other protected classification. This informs and defines the solutions to the employee vs. employer problem discussed in the next section.

## Workplace Compensation Issues

There's one more source of fuel for the employee vs. employer fire: money.

As should by now be evident, employers cannot unlawfully discriminate in their compensation practices—you cannot provide less favorable compensation or benefits to an employee because of gender, race, disability . . . or any other protected classification. Congress added additional penalties for the failure to pay men and women equal pay for equal work by enacting the Equal Pay Act and related laws. Discrimination and Equal Pay Act claims based on compensation differentials are rampant, and they are not so easily avoided— determining when different jobs constitute "equal work" deserving of equal pay can be subjective and unpredictable. One of the most confusing and dangerous compensation issues concerns employees who work overtime.

The overtime issue is covered on the federal level by the Fair Labor Standards Act (FLSA), a piece of New Deal legislation that also covers issues such as child labor and the minimum wage. The FLSA categorizes employees as either "exempt" (those to whom overtime need not be paid) or "non-exempt" (those to whom overtime must be paid). Many states have their own, more stringent overtime laws—most retain the basic FLSA exempt/ non-exempt framework, but for example, some calculate overtime entitlements on a daily basis (instead of using the FLSA's weekly framework), some require that overtime be compensated at more than the time-and-one-half stipulated by

⋯⟩ **One of the most confusing and dangerous compensation issues concerns employees who work overtime.**

the FLSA, some limit the amount of overtime hours employees can be required to work, and some treat certain narrow types of employment categories in a specialized way. Companies are required to comply with the differing laws of each state in which they do business. Each state's Web site provides the details.

Most employers know that if an employee is classified as exempt, no overtime is owing, and if an employee is classified as non-exempt, overtime must be paid if the employee works more than forty hours in a week. Beyond that, there is a comprehensive overtime mythology that leads to colossal liabilities—often through aggressive enforcement proceedings brought by the Department of Labor, often through private lawsuits on behalf of individual employees or groups of employees who have banded together, and often through class actions brought on behalf of hundreds or even thousands of employees at a time. The penalties for failing to abide by the technicalities of the FLSA can be enormous.

My colleagues and I are often asked to make sure that a particular client is complying with overtime requirements. At the onset of the analysis, we'll ask the client's management personnel for a roster of the employees they classify as exempt so we can make sure the client is not failing to pay overtime to an employee who is lawfully entitled to overtime. "Here's the list of salaried employees," they'll tell us. We didn't ask for the salaried employees, we'll respond. We asked for the employees you classify as exempt. Too often, the response is puzzlement. "These are the employees who are paid a salary. Salaried employees don't receive overtime. Only the hourly employees are paid overtime."

No, no, no. The FLSA does *not* define whether an employee is exempt from overtime requirements based on whether an employer chooses to pay the employee a salary. Would that you could escape the obligation to pay overtime to every full-time employee merely by putting the employee on salary, but that's not the way it works.

--> **The FLSA does *not* define whether an employee is exempt from overtime requirements based on whether an employer chooses to pay the employee a salary. Would that you could escape the obligation to pay overtime to every full-time employee merely by putting the employee on salary, but that's not the way it works.**

Deciding who is exempt and non-exempt requires a detailed and specialized analysis. The exempt/non-exempt rubric can work both ways: sometimes an employee you consider to be exempt is really non-exempt and must be paid overtime; but sometimes an employee you consider to be non-exempt is really exempt or can easily be converted to exempt status through a minor change in duties.

The FLSA provides that every employee is entitled to overtime payments unless that employee falls within a defined exception. The primary exception includes so-called white collar employees who fit within the FLSA's "administrative," "executive," or "professional" classifications—if an employee fits within one of those defined categories, the employee is exempt. To qualify, an employee must meet two tests: a salary test *and* a job duties test. The salary test requires that the employee earn at least $455 per week ($23,660 per year). If he doesn't, he will be non-exempt, no matter the job duties. The job duties test is much more complex, but basically, the employee must perform nonmanual duties that involve managerial responsibilities, or the employee must fall within the FLSA's definition of a "professional," which entails employees whose primary duties involve performing work that requires advanced knowledge of a type customarily acquired through extensive education. There are other exceptions, conditions, twists, and turns. The DOL explains the details quite nicely on its Web site—see www.dol.gov/whd/overtime_pay.htm.

THE FOUR MISTAKES

Job descriptions can help a great deal. Suppose you claim an employee fits within the exempt classification, and the DOL thinks otherwise. A written job description showing that the employee has in fact been assigned the requisite amount of managerial authority might tilt the balance in your favor. So will written performance evaluations that describe the management responsibilities the employee in question has actually exercised.

Many employers, again relying on what seems like common sense, will dock not only non-exempt but also exempt employees who fail to work when they're supposed to. You don't have to pay an exempt employee for a morning's work if he doesn't show up until the afternoon, do you? In the arcane world of the FLSA, that's not a simple question. Remember this: you can convert an exempt employee to a non-exempt employee based on the way you treat him. If you dock an exempt employee for hours not worked, the DOL might conclude that the exempt employee is really a non-exempt employee—after all, you're the one treating him like he's a non-exempt employee—and you may then find yourself stuck with a huge overtime obligation that could have been avoided. It's worth asking for some professional help to understand your options and nail down the technicalities.

The FLSA requires overtime be paid to employees who work more than forty hours in a week. That seems like an easy criterion to apply; however, it's anything but. For instance, some employees spend designated periods when they are "on-call"—they're not working, but they have to stay available. Depending on the extent to which the on call responsibility interferes with the employee's personal life, the time spent while on call might be time for which the employer must pay the employee. What about the time employees spend putting on required protective clothing or other gear and the time it takes for an employee to get from the changing area to the work area? That, too, is compensable time counted in the forty hours.

In the hope of avoiding the obligation to pay overtime, many employers will prohibit employees from working more than forty hours per week. Frequently, they will have written policies mandating that overtime is not permitted unless authorized in writing by management. Employees, however, will often work overtime even if it's unauthorized. Sometimes they do it because they are dedicated employees. Sometimes they do it because they are fearful that they will be laid off if they don't. In any event, employers must pay for overtime that they have any reason to know about, *even if the overtime was prohibited*. There's no "I told you not to do it" defense.

> **In any event, employers must pay for overtime that they have any reason to know about, even if the overtime was prohibited.**

Employers are also required to keep detailed records for each employee, including occupation, hours worked daily and weekly, total straight time paid per pay period, and total overtime paid per pay period. The records must be preserved for at least three years.

A substantial amount of FLSA litigation is generated by disgruntled employees who decide to "drop a dime" on an employer who denied them a promotion or laid them off. All an employee needs to do in order to pursue a possible FLSA claim against an employer is make a simple call to the local federal or state DOL office, and if the claim seems credible, you'll find yourself mired in a nightmarish audit. It's worth it, *really* worth it, to make sure you handle the compensation issues correctly.

------

As part of the effort to get his arms around the case, Lou Case assigned one of his young, crackerjack associates, Kent Wynn, to analyze and assess the potential legal issues raised by Owen Moore and his management team. Case read Wynn's memo—its sheer length evidenced the magnitude of the problems he knew he'd be asked to resolve. Case took a deep breath, asked his assistant to e-mail a copy to Moore, and waited for the telephone call.

LOUIS D. CASE AND ASSOCIATES

MEMORANDUM OF LAW

FROM:      Kent Wynn, Esquire

TO:        Louis D. Case, Esquire

CLIENT:    Moore Company

           Client No. 8876-23

SUBJECT:   Analysis of Potential Employee Claims

You requested that I review and analyze the risks posed by the potential claims that present and former employees may bring against our client, Moore Company, as generally referenced in the recent letter from Susan Fairley. As you instructed, I have carefully investigated the facts and researched the law. My conclusions are set forth below:

The claimants include terminated employees as well as employees who are still employed by Moore Company. At the time of the actions in question, they were all employees at-will. Therefore, the issue is whether the client's actions violated any of the various exceptions to the general rule that an employer is permitted to manage and terminate employees at-will as the employer thinks best.

It is clear that the client's actions were motivated by the need to address its dire financial circumstances and not by some unlawful purpose. In view of the client's financial records and the many e-mails and memos exchanged during the period at issue, this will not be difficult to prove.

Nevertheless, there are serious issues that arise from the client's apparent ignorance of the most fundamental laws that regulate the employer-employee relationship. The most important of these issues are detailed below:

Preliminarily, it is important to stress that Moore Company made no serious effort to comply with its obligations under the employment laws. It acted without the advice of counsel. It had established virtually no procedures or policies designed to promote compliance with employment laws. It did not have a complaint and investigation procedure in place as would meet legal standards. It did not train its executives, managers, and supervisors in the effort to ensure that they would not violate the law in their interactions with employees. I am, therefore, fearful that a court will view the client as an employer that dealt with its legal obligations in a reckless way, that the client will lose important defenses, and that any potential damages will be substantially increased as the law permits.

Much of the client's exposure stems from the fact that Owen Moore required Florence Charte, the Production and Distribution Department manager, to reduce the employee count in her department by one-quarter. The client had the right to do that. However, I have interviewed both Charte and Moore, and their statements, as well as the documents they created, evidence a variety of apparent illegalities.

Charte singled out for termination employees who had taken prior FMLA leave. Moore approved of her actions.

This opens the door for a retaliation claim by the affected employees—they will argue that they were singled out for termination because they asserted their protected rights under federal law. Charte and Moore told me that they terminated these employees not because they took FMLA leave in the past, but because of the fear that they would take FMLA leave in the future, and that the company could not bear the cost of such absenteeism. However, neither Charte nor Moore has any facts to support the claim that these employees will take future FMLA leave. They simply assumed, without basis, that those who took leave in the past would take leave in the future and terminated the employees for that reason. This is unlawful. An employer cannot single out an employee for adverse treatment because of the employer's fear (especially, as here, an unsubstantiated fear) that the employee will exercise the right to take FMLA leave, a federally protected right.

Charte, with Moore's approval, also singled out several employees for termination based on their past medical history as opposed to their current job performance. The ADA prohibits discrimination not only against employees with disabilities, but also against those who are "regarded as" being disabled. It appears that Charte and Moore treated these employees as if they were or would be unable to perform the essential functions of their jobs based on medical history alone, without any good faith effort to determine if that was really the case, and weeded them out of the workplace for that reason. That could easily be found to violate the ADA.

Charte and Moore also singled out for termination two employees with physical problems because both of them needed some minor assistance from other employees in order to perform their jobs—one (bad knee) needed another employee to help transport materials up a staircase once or twice a day, and the other (bad back) needed to be relieved from loading-dock duty to which he was assigned for only limited periods. If it is determined that these physical conditions are not serious enough to constitute disabilities under the ADA, then the client would have the right to terminate these employees for the purpose of reducing costs. However, there are recent amendments to the ADA that substantially broaden the types of conditions that will qualify as disabilities for ADA purposes. The full meaning of the ADA amendments has not yet been fleshed out by the courts. In my view, there is a significant risk that a bad knee that prevents stair climbing and a bad back that prevents a person from lifting more than ten pounds will be construed as disabilities under the amended ADA. If this were to occur, the client could have substantial exposure: the evidence indicates that the client terminated employees with disabilities because accommodating their disabilities would cost the client money. This is precisely the kind of conduct the ADA was enacted to prevent.

Charte also dealt with another employee, Bruce Easley, in a way that raises additional ADA issues. Charte admits that she became aware that Easley had physical problems that manifested themselves in his job performance. Easley, fearful that he would be the next to be terminated, did not ask for an accommodation. Typically, an employer does not have to provide an accommodation to a disabled employee unless the employee asks for an accommodation. As a result, Moore Company may be able to defeat Easley's ADA claim. However, a court could conclude that Charte's actions, and the overall, Draconian approach Moore Company took to its employees, were designed to intimidate Easley and others from doing or saying anything that might result in their termination. If it is determined that Easley's condition amounted to a disability under the ADA, the company's approach could raise problems.

Charte, with Moore's approval, also admits that she terminated two employees because they were pregnant, and Charte felt that the company could not afford the future absenteeism that often accompanies the birth of a newborn child. In addition, Charte, with Moore's approval, terminated other women because of her assumption that they would become pregnant in the future. These actions will likely constitute a violation of the Pregnancy Discrimination Act.

The pregnant employees were also given preferential severance packages because of their pregnancies. Men and older employees were given no severance or less favorable severance. This may raise gender and age discrimination issues as well.

Charte, with Moore's approval, terminated two employees, each older than forty, because they were "set in their ways" and because she doubted that they had the energy to work at the pace that would be required after the layoffs were effectuated. There is nothing in the files that pertains to either employee that would support the conclusion that they were inflexible or lacked energy. As such, the decision to terminate them will be characterized as having been based on age stereotypes and nothing more, which is a plain violation of the ADEA. Without some documented basis on which to argue that these employees were terminated because of their job performance as opposed to their age, I do not know how we would successfully defend against this claim.

Charte, with Moore's approval, also terminated two employees she labeled as "complainers" because she assessed them as negative influences who would be likely to damage morale during a time when maintaining morale could be crucial. Generally, an employer would have every right to terminate an employee for this reason. However, both Charte and Moore admit that one of the employees, an African American, was selected because he had filed a prior race discrimination charge against Moore Company. The charge was dismissed, and the employee remains angry about the outcome. Despite the dismissal of the charge, I found no evidence that the employee brought it in bad faith. If the client can prove that it terminated the employee because of his current negative or disruptive conduct, as opposed to retaliating against him for having filed the race discrimination charge, then there would be no liability. However, I checked this employee's file, and there are no adverse evaluations or warnings of any kind.

This makes it more likely than not, in my view, that the employee would prevail in a claim asserting that he was singled out based on his previously filed claim.

The other employee labeled as a "complainer," a female, had complained about hostile work environment sexual harassment. You reviewed that situation and advised the client to reprimand the men who were responsible for the harassment. Since that time, the employee has been shunned and ignored by her fellow employees. She complained about that, but the client never addressed the issues. Once again, no documentation exists that would indicate this employee has failed to perform her job. It, therefore, seems that no matter what the truth is, this employee will be able to make a persuasive case that the reason for her termination was based on retaliation for having made a sexual harassment claim and retaliation for having complained about her treatment thereafter.

There are also other issues, involving other management personnel:

I interviewed the Administration Department manager. For the ostensible purpose of determining which employees were the most productive, he read the sent and received e-mails, including the personal e-mails, of each employee in the department. Moore Company has always allowed its employees to use their office e-mail accounts for personal purposes. Moore Company has never notified its employees that their e-mail accounts are subject to review for purposes of analyzing productivity or for any other purpose. The Administration Department manager confirmed that he reviewed e-mails that dealt with, among other things, the medical, marital, and similar issues of the employees. Moore Company employees may, therefore, gainfully argue that they had a reasonable expectation of privacy when utilizing these e-mail accounts, and that their privacy interests have been violated.

I interviewed the Design Department manager. He admitted that two employees were selected for termination because, while most employees in the department were liberals, these employees were staunchly conservative, and the political arguments had become somewhat heated. He felt that departmental harmony would be better served if this source of friction were eliminated. There is no documentation indicating that the two terminated employees had failed to perform their job duties or that the arguments, however vociferous, had ever interfered with the company's business. Political affiliation and speech are not protected classifications under federal law. My assumption had, therefore, been that, as employees at-will, the client could lawfully terminate these employees on this basis. However, I have researched this issue, and Moore Company is in one of the few jurisdictions that does preclude termination based on political expression. These employees, therefore, would seem to have a viable employment discrimination case.

This manager also advised me that another designer, a Muslim, was terminated because customers were reluctant to work with him based on his religion. The manager stressed to me that neither he nor anyone else at Moore Company was biased against Muslims and that this was strictly a business decision made for the purpose of accommodating the wishes of Moore Company customers. Nevertheless, it is very likely that this employee will succeed in a religious discrimination claim. Being a non-Muslim was not a bona fide job qualification. By acting in this fashion, the client was participating in and encouraging the religious bias of its customers, which is not permitted.

Moore Company employs an extensive sales force that is paid on a salary-plus-commission basis. As part of its cost-savings efforts, Moore Company has unilaterally changed the compensation structure, making it substantially less favorable for the sales personnel. Many of these sales representatives were recruited from other companies, from which they gave up lucrative arrangements. Each of them claims that Owen Moore personally recruited them and told them that if they left their prior employment and came to Moore Company, their compensation package would never be less favorable than the salary-plus-commission arrangement that Moore Company had most recently decreased. Owen Moore denies this. However, Moore Company never bothered to confirm the compensation deal in any form of writing, so we are left with a "my word against your word" issue. At least eight sales personnel will testify that Moore made this promise. As you know, an agreement of this nature can be made orally and need not be in writing. Moore can produce no witnesses to substantiate his recollections. If the personnel version of the facts is believed, the sales representatives will stand to recover well in excess of $300,000 based on the breach of the oral contract.

Lois Price, Sales and Marketing Department manager, engaged in additional, worrisome conduct. One of the sales personnel, Diane Fast, advised her that she wished to have preemptive cancer surgery and requested FMLA leave for that reason. Although elective, Fast had obtained a physician's opinion that the surgery was medically justifiable. Price never asked Fast for any medical information regarding the necessity for the surgery. Instead, Price pressured Fast to forgo the surgery in view of Moore Company's fiscal issues and threatened that she would not hold Fast's position open, as required by the FMLA, unless Fast acceded to Price's demands. Fast did delay the surgery for several weeks but then became distraught and had the surgery. Price then filled Fast's position, which Fast did not find out about until she attempted to return to work. Fast remains unemployed. There is a very good chance that as a result of the foregoing, Fast will recover back pay, future lost pay, and her counsel fees.

The entire situation is further exacerbated by Owen Moore's own conduct. His long-time CFO, Noah Ford, took leave as permitted by the most recent amendments to the FMLA to care for his son who was injured while serving in the military in Afghanistan. Moore did not hold Ford's position open during the leave. Under limited circumstances, an employer may refuse to reinstate highly paid "key" employees, but to do so, it must provide certain notices and satisfy other requirements, none of which Moore Company even attempted to do. Ford will have a viable FMLA claim as a result, and when looking at the claim in full, a court may well view Moore Company as having recklessly violated its employees' FMLA (and other) rights, in which event Moore Company will be assessed a substantial amount of additional liquidated damages.

As noted above, the fact that Moore Company acted throughout this time without the benefit of counsel and without having implemented the proper procedures or training will make it very difficult to contend that Moore Company acted in good faith.

We also must confront serious issues under the FLSA. As you know, the FLSA requires that overtime be paid to non-exempt employees who work more than forty hours per week. Moore Company has been knowingly permitting non-exempt employees to work more than forty hours per week and has not been paying overtime because the employees, fearful they would be included in the next round of layoffs, did not demand it. One or more of the terminated employees has now reported this practice to the DOL, which initiated the usual FLSA audit procedures. Owen Moore told the DOL auditor that he was not paying overtime because all of his employees are salaried. You can imagine the reaction. This matter has all the earmarks that will result in the assessment of not only the back overtime but major penalties.

In other circumstances, Moore Company might have had the opportunity to discuss matters with the employees and work out some kind of reasonable settlements. However, it conducted no exit interviews with its terminated employees and manifested little concern for their well-being. When it paid severance, it obtained no releases in exchange for same. Its extraction of unreasonable hours and effort from its remaining employees without additional compensation or other acknowledgment has created a substantial rift between management and labor. I would not be surprised if employees are beginning to discuss unionization. We should counsel the client immediately with respect to what it can and cannot do in that regard in the effort to head off an additional battery of problems.

In my view, the EEOC (which enforces Title VII and related discrimination issues and the ADA) and the DOL (which enforces the FMLA and the FLSA) will be most interested in aggressively pursuing Moore Company because of the scope and breadth of the violations and the paucity of meaningful defenses. They will assemble the facts, during which Moore Company will be subjected to extremely onerous and time-consuming investigations. The EEOC and the DOL will probably see Moore Company as blatantly disregarding employment laws, and they will want to make an example out of the client.

These agencies, and/or Fairley, will then pursue the various damage actions—and there will be a lot to pursue. Even if the client is ultimately able to prevail on some of the claims, I am not sure this client could afford the cost of defense.

A $100,000+ retainer would be in order. The EEOC and the DOL, to say nothing of Ms. Fairley, will consume huge amounts of our time. Ultimately, taking advantage of whatever protections a bankruptcy can provide may be the best and, perhaps, the only option left.

■ ■ ■

## Creating the Solution:
## Legal Audits, Emergency Repairs,
## Preventive Maintenance, and Red Flags

Now that you know where the primary employee vs. employer hazards are, you can plot an effective strategy by which to avoid them. It's all about the pursuit and achievement of three goals:

First goal: *find out where the most serious problems and deficiencies are.* Different companies have different issues and priorities. The solution needs to be tailored accordingly: first things first; some risks are tolerable, and some, not.

Second goal: *prevent what can be prevented.* There are ways to stop employee vs. employer issues before they start. That is the least expensive and most effective solution. "An ounce of prevention . . ."

Third goal: *make sure those in a position to see the red flags know what they are and how to respond to them.* Not every risk can be forestalled—there *will* be mistakes and problems. What's important is to make sure that the first responders (that is, anyone who manages anyone else, from the top down) know an employee vs. employer red flag when they see one, how to assess the seriousness of the situation, what to do by way of initial and immediate response, and when and where to get help.

In my experience, there's a tried-and-true, four-step program through which these goals can and must be achieved.

## Step One: The Legal Audit

The first step, like the first step in any risk management program, is to identify the risks that most need managing. There's no one-size-fits-all, off-the-rack solution. Over the years, I have come to refer to this step as a legal audit—it's basically a business physical, focusing on the areas from which employee vs. employer claims arise. You'll need to engage the services of someone who knows where to look and who comprehends the significance (or insignificance) of what he finds. Depending on the complexity and size of your business, once a thorough review is done, you should only have to monitor the situation for the next several years.

The most effective approach to a legal audit is to first focus on each significant stage in the chronology of the typical employer-employee relationship. The specifics depend on the nature of the business. The approach will be different depending on whether a company's employees are primarily blue collar or white collar. A distribution company needs to be looked at differently from a consulting company. A company with ten employees needs to be reviewed in a different way from a company with ten thousand employees. But, basically, an effective legal audit will normally analyze the following:

- Recruiting, interviewing, and hiring
- Evaluation and discipline
- Promotion, training, and job assignments
- Employee complaints, problems, and needs
- Termination
- Compensation and pay practices

These are the primary employee vs. employer claim hatcheries. Discrimination claims arise from interview questions, who is hired, who is favorably evaluated and promoted, who obtains sought-after training and job assignments, who is laid off, and so on. ADA issues often arise during the interview process, and ADA and FMLA issues are confronted at all stages thereafter. All manner of issues, such as ADA, FMLA, sexual harassment, and retaliation problems, can be stopped before combustion or fanned into conflagrations depending on how employee complaints and problems are handled and how termination decisions are arrived at and implemented. Compensation and pay practices lead to discrimination issues and FLSA issues.

Some of the questions that have to be asked—generally in some cases and in reference to each aspect of the employment process in others—include the following:

*How sophisticated and complete are the company's policies and procedures?* Whether a company has the proper policies and procedures in place tells me a lot about the executives who run the business—their recognition of the issues, their employment practices sophistication, their commitment to compliance, and so on. For instance, do they control, through policies and procedures and companion forms and checklists, the applicant recruitment and interviewing process, the hiring process, employee evaluation procedures, discipline, compensation issues, termination, exit interviews . . . ? If they do not even go through the motions of attempting to ensure compliance (think Moore Company), that's one thing. If they have at least given it a go, although ineffectively or artlessly, that's something else. If their policies and procedures are top notch, that's another story.

*To what extent are the policies and procedures followed in actual practice?* A high-quality policy-and-procedure manual, complete with forms and checklists, is theory; the extent to which executives, managers, and supervisors understand it and actually do what is required is practice—and much more important. Consistency and uniformity are crucial—do some managers follow the rules, while others ad lib via their own subjective sense of right and wrong?

*What is the claims history?* Have there been prior employee claims? What were the allegations? How were they resolved? Was anything changed as a result? Are the people who were involved still employed?

*What is the nature, quality, and effectiveness of the documentation process?* By now, you know the importance of documentation. A terminated employee claims he was fired because of gender, religion, or some other protected characteristic. Will the company be able to prove the termination was based on poor performance or disciplinary issues? If an employee claims he told a supervisor he needed to take leave to care for his child, and his supervisor claims he said he wanted the week off to go fishing, will the supervisor be able to prove it?

*How well staffed and sophisticated is the human resources department?* A company with a professionalized HR Department needs a much different prescription than a company with employees that think HR is payroll and benefits and little more. It takes a broad and deep knowledge and experiential base to cope with the array of ever-changing employment laws that fuel the employee vs. employer war, while at the same time promoting employee competence, morale, and retention. The lack of an appropriate HR presence is a surefire harbinger of significant problems—it's like a financial system without internal controls or an IT system without virus protection.

*Have executives, managers, and supervisors been trained? How often? By whom?* In the flyover, we discussed the importance of training as a means to preserve legal defenses. The logic is simple. Employees have rights, and employers have the obligation to ensure, to the extent reasonably possible, that the executives, managers, and supervisors who deal with employees will understand and respect those rights. Training is crucial for another reason as well: in the effort to minimize employee vs. employer claims, *it works.* We'll talk about training in more detail later, but the point for now is this: if I'm dealing with a company that has not competently and regularly trained its executives, managers, and supervisors in the employment law principles that pertain to their spheres of influence, I know I'm dealing with a company that is way, way behind the curve.

*Is there a clear and effective procedure in place for handling and investigating potential sexual harassment and other complaints?* If a company has not implemented, and does not consistently respect, a clear complaint and investigation procedure to address harassment and other employment practices issues, it will lose one of the few defenses it has—a defense that might single-handedly win the case. In addition, it will appear to any involved government agency, judge, or jury as if the company simply ignored these issues and should be punished for its crass disrespect for the law.

Think about how you would react if you were a juror in a case in which an employee was injured in a factory accident. During the case, the evidence showed that there were safety hazards that could have been prevented, but the company had no effective channel through which employees could send the message to upper management, and those who did complain were brushed off. Suppose the evidence also showed that after the case, the company did only a cursory investigation to find out what happened in order to prevent other employees from being hurt. How might that affect your judgment when it came time to determine if the company was liable and how much it should pay?

On the other side of this coin, the potential benefits of a proper complaint and investigation procedure cannot be overstated: more and more, courts are refusing to help employees who refuse to help themselves. For instance, in one recent case, a female employee was harassed and then sexually assaulted on three occasions by her supervisor. The company had a clear and proper complaint and investigation procedure in place that had been distributed and made known to the employee, but she did not report the supervisor's conduct at a time when the assaults could have been prevented and waited until after the third incident. The court dismissed her lawsuit based on her failure to use the procedure.

In another case, a male employee was repeatedly propositioned for sex by his female supervisor. The company had the correct policy in place, but the employee failed to use it. His lawsuit was dismissed for that reason. In another case, a female housekeeper at a medical center was grabbed and propositioned by a co-worker. She followed the medical center's complaint procedure and reported the incident immediately. Her employer properly investigated, took the appropriate action, and the harassment stopped. The housekeeper sued—and the court dismissed her complaint because the medical center had the right procedures in place and took the right investigatory and remedial actions as soon as it knew of the problem.

> **The potential benefits of a proper complaint and investigation procedure cannot be overstated: more and more, courts are refusing to help employees who refuse to help themselves.**

Most of these cases arise in the context of hostile work environment sexual harassment cases, but the importance of having a proper complaint and investigation procedure in force is expanding into other kinds of harassment cases as well.

If a company doesn't have the right kind of complaint and investigation procedure in effect, the warning bells start ringing.

*Is there a procedure in place for handling and responding to ADA and FMLA issues?* As discussed in the flyover, ADA and FMLA claims are among the most difficult for employers to "get"—the ADA can force an employer to retain (and spend lots of extra money on) an employee who cannot perform all aspects of his job, and the FMLA can force an employer to hold an employee's job open and continue to pay benefits while the employee takes an extended leave to take care of someone else. ADA and FMLA issues are too difficult and hypertechnical to leave to the best judgment of whoever happens to be on duty when they arise. If I see a company that hasn't as yet recognized this necessity and done what is required to mechanize the process, that tells me something.

*Is there an e-mail policy? Is e-mail monitored? How is the policy enforced?* An employee claims that you fired him based on his race. You assert that you are not a racist and would never make employment decisions based on race—it's just not relevant; it's not something you think about. During the discovery phase of the lawsuit, your e-mails are reviewed, and a variety of e-mails including race-based jokes are unearthed. Imagine the cross-examination.

Companies without e-mail policies that prohibit these kinds of messages are at risk. However, just issuing a policy is not enough—it has to be respected in practice, and it has to be enforced. Still, you'll need to be careful: If you're going to check employee e-mails for compliance with your policy, you need to notify the employees in advance in order to avoid invasion of privacy claims. Check your state and local laws as well—some localities have specialized rules regarding e-mails.

*Are employees properly classified as exempt and non-exempt? Are proper overtime-pay procedures respected?* As mentioned in the flyover, through misinformation and misunderstanding, many companies fail to pay legally mandated overtime to employees who should be classified as non-exempt. Indeed, the Department of Labor has estimated that a substantial majority of companies regularly fail to comply with FLSA requirements. At the same time, many companies pay overtime they don't legally owe.

*Look at the percentages.* Don't forget the dangers inherent in disparate impact claims. Suppose a company draws its workers from a twenty-mile radius. Demographically, that area is 30 percent Hispanic. Only 5 percent of the company's employees are Hispanic. Another company laid off one-third of its workforce. Forty percent of its workers are forty or older, but 60 percent of the laid-off workers were older than forty. None of these facts, by themselves, constitute an illegality, but they most certainly harbor the potential for an illegality, and they need to be investigated.

⇢ **If done right, a legal audit will disclose whether a company's employee vs. employer infrastructure needs to be created from scratch or simply tweaked and refined. It will disclose what kinds of potential claims are more likely to occur than others.**

If done right, a legal audit will disclose whether a company's employee vs. employer infrastructure needs to be created from scratch or simply tweaked and refined. It will disclose what kinds of potential claims are more likely to occur than others. Like a doctor armed with X-rays and test results, once you obtain that crucial diagnostic information, you can tell the difference between what needs to be done right away, where to focus long-term, and what can be left alone.

## Step Two: Fix What Needs Immediate Fixing

The first and most immediate post–legal audit step is triage—fix what needs immediate fixing, the accidents that are about to happen. To continue the medical analogy, stabilize the patient.

For example, if there is no published and posted employee complaint and investigation procedure, that needs to be addressed right away. If non-exempt employees are misclassified or are not being paid in accordance with the FLSA, that needs to be fixed right away. If there is evidence of a hostile work environment involving race, gender, religion, or any other protected class, that needs to be fixed right away. If managers who deal with employees don't understand the basics of an ADA request for a reasonable accommodation or an FLSA request for leave, that needs to be fixed right away. If men are being paid more than women for essentially the same work, that needs to be fixed right away.

## Step Three: Create and Use Preventive Procedures and Forms

Thereafter, when the brush fires are out, the task is to develop customized, minimally intrusive procedures and forms geared toward the prevention of the most significant nascent problems revealed by the legal audit. Those procedures and forms will then be implemented during the fourth step—training.

The idea behind procedures and forms of this nature is to address the riskiest aspects of the employee-employer relationship by removing as much management discretion as is feasible and substituting prescribed courses of action. "Do the following thing in the following way, using the attached form." "If $X$ happens, do $Y$, following the attached procedure and using the attached form." A manager does not have to know all the reasons and nuances behind the procedures and forms (though some basic knowledge will help). If properly designed and effectively and consistently implemented, procedures and forms negate the danger in having nonemployment law experts making employment law decisions that require substantial expertise. This will prevent an array of employee vs. employer issues and, for that reason, these kinds of procedures and forms must become part of a company's infrastructure. They must become standard operating procedure.

As is so frequently the case, however, common sense by itself will not be enough when designing procedures and forms. For instance, as

⇢ **If properly designed and effectively and consistently implemented, procedures and forms negate the danger in having nonemployment law experts making employment law decisions that require substantial expertise.**

detailed previously, every company should focus on creating and implementing a complaint and investigation procedure—but in order to be legally effective, it must include an array of components most companies would not anticipate. For instance, it should not only specify to whom employees should report a complaint, it also should describe what an employee should do if the person designated to receive complaints is himself the subject of a complaint. It should assure employees that there will be no retaliation for a good faith complaint, and it should address issues of confidentiality. Once a complaint is received, it *must* be investigated by a qualified and unbiased individual, all leads must be followed, and all information obtained must be properly documented. This is an area in which you must obtain professional help to make sure you get it right.

Many other aspects of the employee-employer relationship will benefit through the use of procedures and forms. For instance, consider the applicant interviewing process, in which mistakes are all too easily made, especially in companies in which non-HR personnel handles interviews. For instance:

- *"This job will require some heavy lifting. Have you ever had any back problems?"* That's a violation of the ADA. You're allowed to ask whether an applicant can perform the essential functions of a job, but you can't discriminate based on medical history.

- *"McGillicutty? Is that an Irish name?"* The interviewer intended it as innocent small talk, an icebreaker. However, suppose the applicant is not hired and claims his nationality had something to do with it. The interviewer will deny any prejudice. Why, then, the EEOC will ask, were you trying to find out the applicant's nationality?

- *"Most of your co-workers are men. Can you fit in?"* It's a woman's obligation to do the job. It's not her obligation to "fit in" to male behavioral standards. Suppose she answers that she'll do her job, but it's not lawful to ask her to cater to the men in the department. If you don't hire her, you might have to prove that your decision was based on qualifications, not gender discrimination.

- *"You're going to have to change your dress to fit into our dress code."* If the applicant is wearing religious attire, and there's no good reason why it would interfere with the job for which he's interviewing, there will be problems.

- *"Our company has always been nonunion, and we intend to stay that way. Can we trust you to go along with that?"* Major, major issues . . .

An interviewer's notes can be subpoenaed as further evidence of the factors that went into the hiring decision. "Seems a little old for this job." "Said she was thinking of starting a family soon." "Bad facial scar—might turn some people off." All of these notes would give an applicant who claimed foul ample evidence on which to base a lawsuit.

A preventive procedure and companion form for employment interviews can help to keep those who interview applicants from making these mistakes. It gives the interviewer a set of guidelines and a place to take the right kind of notes. If later confronted with an applicant who falsely claims that the interviewer stepped over the employment law line, the procedure will help the interviewer corroborate his side of the story—it shows that he knew where the boundaries were and had been instructed by his employer to stay within them—and the form will provide documentary evidence of compliance.

Forms can be lifesavers in many other contexts as well. Consider a situation in which an employee was refused a promotion based purely on merit. The employee claims that the decision was based on race, gender, age, pregnancy, or another protected trait. If the employee's supervisor was equipped with an employee evaluation procedure and form, taught how to use the form and document the evaluation, and monitored to make sure he consistently complied (as opposed to taking the easy way out and providing only "vanilla" evaluations), there will be a convincing, written performance record that can be effectively used to combat the employee's accusation. Otherwise, the balance tilts strongly toward the employee.

Think about how a clear and simple written procedure that tells a manager what he needs to know—coupled with a form that leads the manager through the required steps and doubles as a documentary record of what was done—could help prevent problems in the following employee vs. employer trouble spots:

- How to recognize an ADA or FMLA issue, how to respond to requests for accommodations or leave, the questions that are and are not allowed, and documenting precisely what was done
- What to do when an employee raises a sexual harassment issue, how to trigger the company's complaint and investigation procedure, and how to document how the complaint was handled
- The warning signs of a hostile work environment, how to react, and how to document the action taken
- What to do when an employee claims that he requires some kind of accommodation based on his religious beliefs and how to document the action taken
- How to select employees for training and job assignments and how to document the basis for the choice
- How to determine if discipline is required, what form of discipline to utilize, and how to document the basis for the discipline
- How to handle absentee issues for exempt and non-exempt employees and how to document the action taken
- The steps to follow when terminating an employee, when and how to conduct an exit interview, and how to document the action taken

## Step Four: Train Executives, Managers, and Supervisors the Right Way

Training is when plans become realities, when talk becomes action. It's great to figure out what needs to be fixed. It's great to develop pristine procedures and forms that home in on the problems. But without training, it all runs the risk of remaining just words coupled with good intentions.

--> **Training is when plans become realities, when talk becomes action.**

As mentioned previously, in some jurisdictions, management training is statutorily or judicially mandated; you'll be fined—or worse—if you don't provide it on a regular basis. Even in jurisdictions in which the failure to train is not a punishable offense, training is mandatory as a practical matter: the liability risks associated with allowing untrained managers in the workplace are simply too great. The logic underlying these policies is unassailable. Just as employers are not permitted to allow an untrained forklift driver or crane operator in the workplace, employers cannot allow an untrained manager in the workplace. Either way, employees are endangered—in the former context, their safety is endangered; in the latter context, their rights are endangered.

There's no one right way to train executives, managers, and supervisors in the art of minimizing employee vs. employer risks, but in my experience, the training should focus on two key skills. Before you settle on a trainer, review his training protocol with this in mind:

*First: red flag recognition.* You cannot make a group of managers into employment law experts in a three-hour training session; if it seems that the trainer will focus primarily on employer-employee dos and don'ts and the elements of an ADA claim and a sexual harassment defense, get another trainer. Explaining the key points of employment law lends important context, but the foundation of the training must be red flag recognition—how to tell the difference between the routine and the dangerous, between what can be overlooked and what must be stopped in its tracks. This is where it has to start: the ability to recognize a potential problem is a prerequisite to the ability to prevent a potential problem.

An employee tells his supervisor that he's got a bad back and needs some help. A manager sees a poster in an office cubicle that demeans women or an ethnic group. An employee asks the COO for two months off during a company's busy season to take care of his mother. A department head notices that an employee keeps staying late but is not putting in for overtime. The right kind of training will illuminate these kinds of events and circumstances and show them for what they are—opportunities to turn potential problems into nonevents.

*Second: what to do in the first fifteen seconds.* Once an executive, manager, or supervisor recognizes a red flag, he must *immediately* respond in the right way—a great many employee vs. employer claims are rooted in the first fifteen seconds of the initial employee-employer exchange. Training has to concentrate on that first, critical management response: the wrong response makes it much more likely that the employee will ultimately bring a claim and that the claim will have merit; the right response not only diminishes the likelihood of a claim, it also diminishes the legal underpinnings of whatever claim the employee may choose to file.

> ⇢ **A great many employee vs. employer claims are rooted in the first fifteen seconds of the initial employee-employer exchange. Training has to concentrate on that first, critical management response.**

One of the most valuable sentences an executive, manager, or supervisor can be taught to utilize during the first fifteen seconds is this: "I'll get right back to you." In the face of a known danger, appreciate that common sense may not be the answer, keep things as they are, and check with the experts.

An employee with a history of baseless complaints and malingering tells his supervisor that he's got a blood-sugar problem, and he needs an extra break. The supervisor sees the ADA red flag but, knowing whom he's dealing with, tells the employee that he needs to focus on doing his job, not taking more time off. The employee is angry and now has the makings of a claim. *Or*, the supervisor holds his tongue, asks some questions to gather the details, tells the employee he'll get right back to him, and turns it over to HR for further guidance. HR instructs the supervisor to have the employee fill out the appropriate forms so his condition can be investigated and verified; to advise the employee that if it is determined that he does have a medical problem, the company will at that time discuss further options with him; and to confirm the conversation with a memo. The employee knows he's being taken seriously, but at the same time, he gets the message that he's not going to be able to fake a disability. And the company has covered and documented its legal bases.

An employee says she's upset because some of the men keep "hitting on me and refuse to let me be." Her manager sees the red flag and tells her he'll make sure the men knock it off. She perceives it as a brush-off and starts to think that her only alternative is to talk to a lawyer. *Or,* the manager tells her that the company will not tolerate sexual harassment, and he'll get right back to her. In accordance with company policy, the manager calls the Attorney Hotline the company has set up, and is instructed to initiate the company's complaint and investigation procedure. The employee receives a written acknowledgment of her complaint and an outline of the investigative steps that will follow. The employee knows that real efforts are being made to get to the bottom of the problem, and the company has preserved the legal defenses the law provides.

There are, in addition, certain approaches and philosophies that seem to work best in this kind of management training.

*Fear—a surefire attention-getter.* Management personnel often enter these kinds of training sessions with dread—they anticipate two hours of political correctness instruction and nothing of bottom-line value.

The best way to attack that mind-set and focus their attention is to show them actual cases in which skilled and successful managers—people just like them—made decisions that seemed routine and reasonable, only to be crushed with six- and seven-figure verdicts, embarrassing publicity, and ruined reputations. This "there but for the grace of God go you" message makes a not-so-subtle-but-necessary point:

there really is an employee vs. employer war; it's got nothing to do with political correctness; and learning how to win the war is all about saving money and careers.

*Use customized examples.* Examples are the best way to train management personnel in these critical recognition and response skills. However, the training loses all credibility unless the examples sound familiar and ring true. Using stock examples about interactions between a foreman and a machine operator when training department heads in a software firm won't do it.

The trainer should use situations that have actually arisen or are likely to arise in the trainees' workplace—the goal is to produce a "this really could happen here" response and an occasional knowing, or even guilty, smile. The trainer must also use the right lingo—call the departments and positions by their right names, refer to the products or services the company sells in some detail, and so on. This approach obviously takes more time and costs more than using a "canned" training package. But the training will be much less effective if the attendees are prone to see it as a generic exercise, something they are made to do but that has little application to the problems they actually face.

*Teach the company's procedures and forms.* As an ideal, the company will have created the requisite preventive procedures and forms before the training. That's not mandatory, but it helps. When the trainer talks about a sexual harassment example, it's useful to put the company's actual complaint procedure on the screen and use it to explain what the manager ought to be doing. When the trainer goes through the ADA and FMLA scenarios, he can use the company's actual forms as the basis for explaining what the manager should ask the employee, should not ask the employee, and so on. This helps to bring a company's procedures and forms to life and tie the content of the training to the actual workplace in which the managers must function.

*Keep it small, and segregate management levels when possible.* In this kind of training, developing a dialogue between the trainer and trainees is extremely important. You want those in attendance to ask "what if" questions—that's the best way to adapt the content of the training to the real world of those in the room. Limiting the number of people in the session helps this happen. I've found fifteen to thirty people to be about the right range.

Also, depending on the size of the company, it can be important to segregate the top executives from the lower management levels. A customized training program will stress some things to top executives that would never be mentioned to lower-level managers—the trainer has to be careful not to turn the training into an instructional manual for bringing a claim against the company.

THE BEST WAY TO WIN THE EMPLOYEE VS. EMPLOYER WAR IS, of course, to avoid it or, at least, to confine it to limited and occasional scuffles of minor consequence. That's not an easy task. It takes the expertise and will to purge certain old ways of doing business and substitute certain new and reengineered ways of doing business, some of which will not make sense at the onset.

Another part of the solution is to change the predominant employee mindset about employee vs. employer lawsuits. Ambrose Bierce, an early twentieth-century humorist, defined a lawsuit as "a machine which you go into as a pig and come out of as a sausage." That has not always been the case for employees who sue their employers, and that reality, that there may well be a pot of gold at the end of the employee vs. employer rainbow, has fed the monster. Employers need to create a new workplace reality in which employees understand that an ugly, lengthy, draining employee vs. employer lawsuit will probably be more trouble than it's worth. Employers need to do what's necessary so that employees start to understand the wisdom in Bierce's message.

# CHAPTER THREE

# The Third Mistake: Giving Away the Secrets of Your Success

Economists now use terms such as *knowledge capital, knowledge assets,* and *intangible assets* to describe the primary resources successful companies utilize to create revenue. For a variety of sociological and technological reasons, capitalism has changed: it used to be about who amassed the most plants, equipment, and raw materials; now, so much of our commerce is founded on assets that have no physical embodiment in the usual sense. It's the inventions, the techniques, the designs, the innovations, the contacts, and the data that comprise the *real* means of production for most companies, from small proprietorships to the Fortune 100.

This new paradigm, however, comes with new rules. Those who best understand how to use these new rules to their advantage will have the greatest opportunity to succeed.

## Understanding the Problem: Competition vs. Protectionism

In this new kind of capitalism, most successful companies predicate their success on better ideas, not more assets. They outthink rather than outspend their competition. They find a way to deliver superior products and services, and they do it faster and cheaper. They develop creative techniques to penetrate new markets in new ways. They create demand.

Sometimes it comes from new ways to leverage the power of the Internet. Sometimes it's all about a breakthrough in the fundamentals—a "must have" product innovation or a more efficient manufacturing process. Sometimes companies find ways to recruit and retain people who have the knowledge and skill to outperform the competition's people. Sometimes it results from an innovative brand-building strategy. It's the better idea, not the biggest factory, that wins.

These are the primary secrets of success in the twenty-first century. But they are paired with companion conundrums. Once you develop and begin to capitalize on your secrets of success, how do you keep the competition from taking them or imitating them? How can you position yourself so that you, not they, extract the value from what you've created?

Our economic system is founded on the bedrock notion that competition is a good thing. Through a Darwinian struggle among competing businesses, the public has a choice of the best competition-tested products and services at the best possible price.

However, promoting innovation, the free enterprise system's oxygen, also militates in favor of anticompetitive protectionism. Would you invest all of the time, money, and stomach lining required to invent a better mousetrap if, when all is said and done, another company could duplicate it and reap the profits? Innovators need the right to capitalize on what they create; without an incentive, a protected pot of gold at the end of the rainbow, innovation dies.

Still, how far can that kind of protection be taken before innovation is stifled and society begins to suffer? Progress moves forward in steps, with today's innovators building on the work of yesterday's innovators. Today's software designers and bio-mechanical engineers stand on the shoulders of yesterday's software designers and biomechanical engineers. Today's writers and artists develop new works based on what yesterday's writers and artists accomplished. Today's two-pixel digital camera, fifty-thousand-mile tire, and PowerPoint lecture become tomorrow's ten-pixel digital camera, one-hundred-thousand-mile tire, and interactive Web-based training program—*if* we dial down the protectionist side of the policy equation and let it happen.

It's the law's job to strike a balance between these competitive and protectionist interests and establish the rules of engagement. Even the framers of our Constitution recognized how important it was to protect and, therefore, spur innovation—but only to a point. They authorized Congress "to Promote the Progress of Science and the useful Arts, by securing for limited Times to Authors and Inventors the exclusive Right to their respective Writings and Discoveries." Not for all time, but only "for limited Times." As the nature of society and technology continued to change, so did the way that our lawmakers struggled to find the appropriate point of equilibrium.

The upshot is a body of legal rules that defines what's yours and what's not yours, and how you can keep what's yours from becoming someone else's. You've heard the terminology—copyright, patent, trademark, trade secret, nondisclosure, noncompetition, and so on. Do you really know how it all affects your efforts to carve out a niche and take advantage of it? You come up with some new features and enhancements on your doodad that your customers love. You give it a nifty name—the DooMorDad—and use that in your marketing efforts. You develop written materials that show your customers how they can use more doodads in their business. You find and develop a relationship with a supplier or subcontractor that gives you a leg up. Over time, you develop a customer list that includes your key contacts and their buying preferences. You work with your sales manager to develop relationships with your customers. You hire a consultant to develop an expanded business plan, and you implement it. And you succeed.

What stops your competition from putting the same features and enhancements on their doodads? Can they market their doodads as DooMorDads? How about DoMoreDads? Can they go after your customers and use your written materials or something similar? Is there any way to stop them from making a deal with your supplier or subcontractor? Can they recruit your sales manager and ask him to bring along the customer list? Can they ask him to share his knowledge of your customers? Can they get your consultant to develop the same kind of

→ **Success paints a target on your back. To be able to capitalize on what you've worked for and created, you need to understand if, and how, the law will let you keep what's yours. And just as important, you need to understand if and how you can take what's theirs.**

expanded business plan for them? Can they hire your employees, the ones who know about and are working with the new business-development plan?

Success paints a target on your back. To be able to capitalize on what you've worked for and created, you need to understand if, and how, the law will let you keep what's yours. And just as important, you need to understand if and how you can take what's theirs.

---

## The Case of Lester Werk vs. Owen Moore

Grant Little, Goode Manufacturing's lending officer, riffled through the financial statements and smiled. "Owen, your gross receipts are up 40 percent and your net profits are up 55 percent. What in the world is going on?"

Usually, Owen Moore hated these quarterly loan review meetings, but he didn't mind this one. "I'm telling you, Grant. Going into business with Lester Werk was the best move Moore Company ever made."

"I knew you'd turn this around, Owen. I'm happy for you. I've got no problem with your request. We'll bump your line of credit to $2 million and approve the $800,000 term loan. We'll keep the security interest on inventory and receivables in place and hold your $1 million CD as additional collateral and review where we are in three months. OK?"

"Done deal. Thanks, Grant. Werk and I will focus all we have on this product. Green is where it's at. Green will produce green, I promise."

Lester Werk and Owen Moore had been college fraternity brothers. Werk was a graduate engineer and brilliant tinkerer who, politically and emotionally, had never left the '60s, and his life centered on helping

Mother Earth, as he still called it. They remained casual friends and saw each other at annual reunions and occasional dinners, where Werk would unfailingly regale Moore with his views on the future of alternative energy sources.

"You're a natural businessman, Owen. I'm a dreamer. I understand that. But people are starting to understand just how important it is to limit greenhouse gases and achieve clean, renewable energy independence. There will come a day when the American people will buy into the alternative energy concept in droves. You need to get into this early."

"I hear you, Les. But until it makes short-term economic sense for Joe Sixpack, it's not happening. When you come up with something that makes people feel good about the environment *and* puts money into their pocket, call me, and I'll back you to the hilt. Until then, I'm a cynic."

Werk grinned. "I'm going to hold you to that promise, Owen. Maybe sooner than you think."

Three months later, Moore got an e-mail. "Owen—Want to get rich and save the world at the same time? Meet the P2P. Saturday, my place, noon. You bring the beer. Les."

Werk opened the door to his apartment just as Moore was about to knock. "Thanks for coming, Owen. I really, really appreciate it. Today is the first day of the rest of your investment portfolio."

"I haven't seen you this excited since the first Earth Day, Les."

"Follow me, and don't trip. I cancelled my insurance. Do you know what those companies use our premiums to invest in?" Moore stepped over an array of motors and wires, marveling at the different paths they had taken—Moore, the button-down businessman; Werk, the '60s throwback, an unapologetic pursuer of causes. Moore followed Werk into his kitchen.

"Say hi to my baby, Owen. Meet the P2P. And don't laugh until you've given me a chance to amaze and confound you."

Moore's initial reaction reminded him of when he had to feign admiration for his daughter's elementary school watercolors. "OK, Les. Tell me about it."

Through an open window, sitting on an outdoor deck, Moore saw a cylinder the size of an office wastebasket with what looked like a vertical propeller on top, covered in a shiny corrugated film. A cable ran from the cylinder, through the window, and into the back of the dishwasher. Another cable ran from the back of the dishwasher to some sort of meter mounted on the wall.

"Here's the deal, Owen. I understand that most people aren't going to disconnect from the power grid. But suppose there was a device they could buy that would cut their electric bills way down, pay for itself within two years, provide an independent power source when they need it, look cool, and make them feel good about helping the environment?"

"And you're going to tell me that miniature R2D2 out there with the windmill on its head is going to do that, right? Do I get a Veg-o-Matic if I call in the next ten minutes?"

"You've been corrupted by The Man, Owen."

"I *am* The Man, Les."

"I'm going to save you, Owen. What you're looking at is the most efficient wind turbine that's ever been invented. It took me six years to develop it. The film on the outside of the cylinder is actually an incredible breakthrough in solar-panel technology. Inside the cylinder is a state-of-the-art battery arrangement that efficiently stores the electricity the turbine and solar panel produce. And the whole enchilada comes in at fourteen pounds and less than three feet high. You can kiss my ring later."

"I'm listening."

Werk turned on the dishwasher. "The meter on the wall measures the electricity coming from your friendly power conglomerate. It will normally read ninety to one hundred for a dishwasher. What's it reading, Owen?"

"About twenty-five."

"Correct. A stupendous savings. Guess where the rest of the electricity is coming from."

"R2D2, I assume?"

"Right on. The P2P sits on my deck and creates electricity out of sun and air, all for free. I save at least 50 percent on my dishwasher consumption. On sunny and windy days, the percentage is even higher. It's got a circuit that automatically ratchets down power-grid consumption when the P2P is charged up, which is almost always."

Moore's wheels were turning.

"Even better, Owen, I've got another little guy on the roof that does the same thing for my hot water heater and two more in the back that do a bang-up job on my baseboard heat. You hardly notice the little buggers, until you get your electric bill. You're starting to think numbers, aren't you, Owen?"

"I'm still listening."

"The guy who makes the film that acts as the solar panel is a good friend, and we made a pricing deal in exchange for my commitment to stick with him as we grow. The rest of it is all know-how, not materials. You can outsource the machining and assembly so there's minimal capital investment. Maybe it costs you $100 per unit from raw materials to out-the-door. You can sell it for $300, probably more. It'll be a standard feature in new home construction and rehabs. Every apartment owner who has a balcony and pays for his own electricity will want one. Then there's the office buildings . . . and on and on and on."

"This is pretty amazing, Les. This really works?"

"I've already got a certification from the testing lab at our beloved alma mater—each P2P can save $150 to $300 per year in electric bills, easy. You can't afford *not* to buy it. Plus there will be tax credits, electric company rebates, you name it. Patent pending—I filed it myself. Owen, you are looking at the leading edge of the next big thing you business types are always searching for—the green revolution."

"I didn't expect anything like this, Les. I need time to think. Can you be in my office Monday morning to talk business?"

"I'll wear my best Earth Day T-shirt, Owen."

"I was afraid of that. By the way, Les, you've got a device that provides free electricity to anyone who wants it. What's with the goofy P2P name? I need to get my marketing people on that."

"No deal, Owen. The P2P stays the P2P."

"OK, I'll bite."

"P2P—Power to the people, Owen. Finally. Power to the people."

Werk took in the marble conference table and leather chairs in Moore's office with proletarian bemusement.

"I've had my technical people put the P2P through its paces, Les. It's everything you said it was. Let's make this happen. We need to get our lawyers together to work out a business arrangement."

"Sure. While I'm at it, I'll send over my wardrobe manager and personal masseuse. What's next? I have my people call your people, and we do lunch?"

"I'm serious, Les. Business is business."

"I'm serious too, Owen." Werk's face hardened. "Let's get this straight. This is *not* just business to me." He sat down, grimacing. "I'm sorry, Owen. But your world is not my world. We either trust each other, or we don't. I'm OK with a handshake. I can't function in a world of wherefores and whereases. I'll sign what you say I need to sign. But please, let's keep this on a human level."

Moore tried to warm things up. "Sorry for the bad vibes, Les." It didn't help. Werk stared at the floor.

"OK, Les. We'll do this your way for now. I'll tell my lawyer to put a bare-bones, two-page deal together. We'll do everything on a fifty-fifty basis, no complications. We'll form P2P Enterprises. We'll each own half, and we'll split the profits. Your responsibility will be to contribute the P2P technology to the company and take responsibility for the technology- and product-development side. You'll continue fine-tuning this baby and work your butt off doing what you do. My responsibility will be to run anything to do with the business side and work my butt off doing what I do. We'll meet weekly and work out the rest as needed. You comfortable with that?"

Werk held out his hand. "Let's go change the world, Owen."

The next morning, Moore met with his lawyer, Louis D. Case. Moore explained his plans, and Case explained the risks. "I know you're looking out for my best interests, Lou. But you need to minimize this. I really do trust him."

"How about some trust with verification, Owen?"

"Not yet, Lou. I can't. I promised Les it would be as close to a handshake deal as I could make it. Just form a limited liability entity owned equally by Les and me, and put together an operating agreement between us like I told you—he runs the technology, I run the business."

"Owen, please, we'd all like things to be simple, but sometimes, it just can't work that way. What happens if there's a deadlock? What happens if one of you doesn't do your job? What happens if one of you decides to leave or dies or becomes disabled? How will you deal with customers and vendors? What if the company takes off, and people start trying to steal what you have? This is like building a house and deciding to eliminate the foundation because it's 'too complicated.'"

"Maybe later, Lou. You've done your job. Just do what I ask, please."

"You're heading into an ocean with a leaky boat, Owen. I need to protect my firm. I'll send you a letter confirming that you really want to do things this way, OK?"

"As you well know, Lou, I get that. No problem. Hopefully, in a year or so Les will be more comfortable with the business side, and we can get the right documents in place."

"Hopefully, the boat will not have sunk in the meantime. Bon voyage, Owen."

Six months later, Moore was thinking a lot more about meeting demand than dealing with lawyers—P2P Enterprises was stunningly successful.

It took Moore about six weeks to finalize the financing, sourcing, and manufacturing connections—the cost to produce and ship the P2P came in at between $85 to $90 per unit. Werk spent his time in a leased workshop and warehouse, where his passion for the P2P led to substantial size and weight reductions, a 10 percent increase in wind turbine efficiency, a much higher battery storage capacity, and a significant reduction in manufacturing costs.

Once they finalized the logistics and design, Moore and Werk agreed on a start-up marketing strategy that focused on the development of a glitzy Web site with an e-commerce component, a logo and marketing approach focused on the "Power to the People" slogan, and a public relations consultant to generate construction industry trade journal articles. The first orders came from individual homeowners. Residential builders and home improvement companies quickly followed. Big-box stores started to call. Werk came up with a variety of commercial applications, and small-office and light-industrial building owners jumped on the bandwagon.

Werk had been right: the P2P sold itself. The problem was meeting, not creating, demand.

"I hereby call to order the meeting of the board of P2P Enterprises. I shall now take attendance. Are you here?"

"I'm here, Les."

"Excellent. I'm here too. Another superb showing by the board. What's on the agenda, Owen?"

"Les, we need to talk seriously. I'm worn out. I've got my own business to take care of and I'm spending fifty hours a week on P2P. You look completely frazzled as well."

"Too true. I actually slept here two nights last week. I'm losing my free-spirit credentials. What's the solution?"

"I've seen too many businesses become victims of their own success—they create a demand and then fail to satisfy it. We're getting close to that line."

"I can see that."

"We need to hire someone to take responsibility for the day-to-day nitty-gritty. We both have to move into supervisory roles in our own areas of expertise. You've got a dream of distributing hundreds of thousands of P2Ps. I've got a dream of making a ton of money from your dream. We need to start developing the infrastructure to make that happen. This is the first step."

"That's a scary proposition." Werk stood up and looked out the window. "But I'm starting to forget where I live. So I guess I'm willing to try. But I'm not hiring just anybody, Owen. We keep plugging until we find the right person, no matter how long it takes."

"I've already got someone in mind. He'll be here tomorrow for an interview."

William Leavitt had worked for Moore Company for three years. He had an undergraduate degree in electrical engineering, and Moore hired him the week after Leavitt got his MBA. Moore saw his potential early on— Leavitt was independent but knew where the limits were. He was smart, knowledgeable, detail-oriented, and relentless. In addition, he was very unhappy. Moore had taken him out for lunch several weeks before, trying to home in on what it would take to keep Leavitt in the Moore Company fold. Leavitt wasn't shy. "I appreciate everything you've done for me, but I can't be a cog in a wheel, Owen. Moore Company will succeed because of what *you* do. What *I* do doesn't matter all that much. I need to have the opportunity to make something succeed."

"Les, meet Will Leavitt. Will, meet Les Werk."

"Nice to meet you, Will. Come with me."

Werk and Leavitt drove away. Four hours later, Werk showed up at Moore's office.

"He's what we need, Owen. He's half me and half you. He understands what's important. He truly believes in what we're doing. He's the guy."

"That's it? What happened to the 'we're not hiring just anybody' speech?"

"I made a deal with him, Owen, subject to your approval. It's a handshake deal—don't let your lawyers screw up the relationship: $125,000 salary plus benefits. And he gets 10 percent of whatever we decide to take out of the business for ourselves on top of our base salaries. No funny business with defining 'profits'—he gets a piece of what we get."

"Makes sense. My, my. Do I see an emerging capitalist?"

"I only *look* stupid. You read spreadsheets, Owen. I read people. Hire him. Now. No mumbo jumbo. Make it happen. Please. He has the time and energy to make the P2P what it can be. He has the time and energy to make both of our dreams come true. This is a turning point."

Werk was, again, right. Leavitt was a perfect fit. Leavitt handled the details and logistics of production, marketing, and sales. He hired the right staff, implemented the right systems, managed growth, developed opportunities—the more responsibility he was given, the better he did and the happier he was. Moore and Werk stayed very involved, Moore focusing on overall strategy and financial management issues, Werk on manufacturing and performance improvements. On Leavitt's first anniversary, Moore and Werk took Leavitt to dinner and, over a bottle of Dom Perignon, bumped his salary to $175,000 and increased his profit share to 15 percent. Year two went even better than year one.

"Will, there's a Mr. Guy on line one for you."

Leavitt kept reading a sales report while he picked up the telephone.

"Will, this is Richard Guy. I'd like to make you a proposal."

"Mr. Guy, please send us your literature and proposal. I'll have the appropriate people take a look and get back to you if we're interested."

Guy chuckled. "I'm not trying to sell you anything, Will. I am the Guy of Guy International. We're just down the street. Perhaps you've heard of us."

Leavitt stopped reading the sales report. Guy International was a local success story. Richard Guy was a young entrepreneur who built his company from scratch and, in less than ten years, amassed a huge fortune, rumored to be in excess of $100 million. Guy International employed about one hundred people at its local facility and maintained eight international locations. Guy was frequently discussed in Leavitt's MBA classes and was widely admired for his guts, savvy, community involvement, and philanthropy. In many ways, Guy was who Leavitt wanted to be.

"What can I do for you, Mr. Guy?"

"Call me Rich, please. As I said, I have a proposal. I hope you can take an hour or two to talk about it. Would 9:00 A.M. on Friday in my office work for you?"

"I can do that . . . Rich. One thing I've learned is that it never hurts to listen. Can you give me some idea of what you'd like to talk about so I can be certain I'm prepared?"

"You're prepared, Will. Trust me on that."

"I'll look forward to meeting you."

"Will, one more thing."

"Yes?"

"I ask that you don't discuss this with Mr. Moore or Mr. Werk just yet. The reasons for that will become clear when we meet."

Leavitt, uncharacteristically dressed in a dark suit, told the receptionist who he was. "Ah, yes. Rich told me you were coming over. He'll be right down." The receptionist calls him "Rich"? Guy appeared a minute later, dressed in khakis and a T-shirt. He smiled and held out his hand. "Thanks so much for making the time to see me, Will. I know you're busy. Let's go to my office and get right to it."

Guy's office was, at best, spare—standard-issue desk, small conference table and chairs, a couple of family pictures, and piles of papers and files. Everything about Guy seemed strictly utilitarian—all business, no ego. Leavitt loosened his tie and relaxed.

"I apologize for the mess, Will. I've been overseas, and the work keeps piling up faster than I can get to it."

"I know the feeling."

"I know that you do. Which brings me to why I asked you to come over."

Guy pulled out a chair for Leavitt at the conference table and sat down across from him.

"Will, I've looked very carefully at the work you've been doing over at P2P Enterprises. It's hard not to notice how successful that company has become since you became involved."

Leavitt put on his best business face, unsure about where this was going.

"I know a great deal about you, Will. I know every course you took and every grade you achieved at college and in business school. I've spoken to several of your professors. I've had my people study the manufacturing improvements you've made at P2P and how you've improved the marketing and distribution. I've got some pretty reliable information about how that company has grown over the last year."

Leavitt tried to remain expressionless.

"Come with me for just a minute, if you would."

Guy took him through a side door and into a large work room. Eight P2Ps sat on a long bench, in varying states of disassembly. "I have an excellent engineering staff. As you can see, we're pretty familiar with the P2P. It's a brilliantly simple device, very easy to reverse engineer. We know how it works. We know how it's manufactured. We know how much it costs P2P to produce. We have some ideas and some sourcing connections. We think we can produce it faster, better, and for half of what it costs you."

"I'd be interested in hearing more about that."

Guy smiled, walked over to a small metal desk in the corner, and picked up a large file with a variety of subfolders in it. "You'd be equally interested in this, Will. It's the patent application filed by Mr. Werk and some other materials from our intellectual property attorneys."

"And?"

"From all accounts, Mr. Werk is a fine person and a brilliant engineer. I'd love to meet him. But he's no patent lawyer. Three years before he filed this patent application, Mr. Werk began sending detailed copies of the

P2P plans and specs to a variety of organizations—engineering societies, organizations promoting green energy, and so on. He gave at least three presentations." Guy pulled three folders from the file. "Here are the PowerPoint slides he used."

"Les has been proselytizing for a long time. I'm sure of that."

"Understandable, Will. But his proselytizing invalidated his patent application. Once he put the details out for all to see, patent law requires that he file the patent application within a year. Unfortunately for him, and you, he didn't do that. The patent will never be granted. The P2P is in the public domain."

Leavitt saw the writing on the wall. "What are you telling me, Rich?"

"Let's go back to my office."

Leavitt sat down. Guy stood. "Will, here's the business reality. Guy International is going to go into the P2P business. Looks like we can even use the P2P name—Mr. Moore and Mr. Werk never bothered to trademark anything. My lawyers are working on that. The unit will look the same, we'll produce it more cheaply, we'll sell it at a much lower price, and we'll market it on an international basis. You won't beat us. Are you interested in joining us?"

Leavitt tried, unsuccessfully, to remain expressionless.

"I know you must feel a significant loyalty to Mr. Moore and Mr. Werk. I respect you for that. But you're a young man. You do need to think about your future. I can assure you that inside of a year, you won't be working for Mr. Moore or Mr. Werk anyway—with you or without you, P2P Enterprises will no longer be in business."

Leavitt measured his words. "As I said when we spoke, it doesn't hurt to listen."

"Will, I need to ask you some questions before we go further."

"Alright."

"Do you have an employment agreement?"

"No. Les likes to do everything on a handshake, no formalities."

"You didn't sign a covenant not to compete, a nondisclosure agreement, nothing like that?"

"No, nothing."

"Excellent. Does P2P have a customer list that shows the identities of buyers, what they bought at what price, and so on?"

"Sure. It's on the computer. I'm the one who put it together, and I maintain it."

"Again, excellent. Is the customer list kept in confidence—that is, is it secured from those who don't need to see it? Is it protected in any way?"

"Actually, most of it was just put onto our Web site—our marketing people told us it would give us more credibility. Inside the office, everything is pretty much open. It's a Word document. Everybody in the office has access to just about everything."

"Do you have any written agreements with your suppliers and subcontractors?"

"No. Never saw the need for that."

"Will, do you know who supplies you with the solar film? We've had some trouble duplicating that."

"Sure. I know him."

Guy sat back. "Will, I'm overworked. I need people like you. In exchange, I can give you an opportunity to run a division of Guy International. I'll give you a piece of the upside and protect you against the downside." Guy handed him a manila envelope. "It's all in there. Look at it. Have your lawyer look at it. I can assure you that it is exceedingly generous. Let me know if you have any questions or issues, and we'll discuss them. But please let me hear from you within a week."

"I'll do that, Rich."

"Will, I know you've got misgivings. But P2P is a business, not a fraternity. And it won't be a business for long. You're not the captain. It's not your job to go down with the ship."

Werk was pacing, waving his arms. "He can just do that? We were all in this together. We shared everything with him. Yesterday, he was our friend.

Today, he can be our enemy? There's no law against that? Betrayal is legal in this country?"

Lou Case did everything he could to stifle the "I told you so" that was aching to roll off his tongue.

Moore and Werk had arrived at the P2P office mid-morning and found Leavitt's desk, usually a maelstrom of papers and files interlaced with Styrofoam cups and telephone message slips, eerily empty, save for a three-ring binder and an envelope. They opened the envelope, found Leavitt's handwritten note, and called Case.

Owen and Les—

There's no easy way to do this, so here goes. I've decided to leave the company. There's really no choice. Richard Guy contacted me and told me that he's going to start to produce his own P2Ps. He claims that he's got a team of lawyers who say the patent is invalid, and I'm convinced he's got the resources to out-manufacture and out-sell us. I'm at a point in my life where I can't afford a résumé entry that says I helped to run a failed business. Guy offered me the opportunity to run his P2P division. The compensation package and guarantees were something I could not pass up. I had to go with my head and not my heart.

I know this sounds hollow, but I can't thank you enough for the opportunity you gave me. I could not bring myself to do this face to face. Though I know I've done the right thing, it still hurts.

I've organized everything you need to know about what I was handling in the binder. You'll see that it's all here. You won't miss a beat, and if you have any questions, call me—assuming you're still willing to talk to me. I'll understand if you'd rather that I fall off a cliff. I wish things didn't have to turn out this way. But Guy is about to run you over, and I have to protect my future. Like Owen always says, "business is business."

"This happens all the time, Les," Case began. "Employees have the right to leave their employers and go into competition with them. That's the nature of the free enterprise system. You could have stopped Will from doing that or at least made it a lot more difficult. But you wanted to do things based on trust. Sometimes that works, sometimes it doesn't."

"What about my patent? I filed it myself. No one from the patent office ever said there was anything wrong with it. They can knock off the P2P, and there's nothing we can do?"

"I'm sorry, Les. None of this stuff is simple. You put the P2P into the public domain years before you filed for the patent, so you lost your rights. You might have been able to get some protection after you and Owen got together by filing patents on the additional improvements and innovations you made to the original design. But you didn't."

"So Leavitt gets bought off by Guy. And Leavitt can tell Guy everything there is to know about our suppliers, our manufacturers, our customers, our distributors, our marketing, our plans, what works, what doesn't. Guy can steal the P2P from me and use his resources to underprice us. And there's nothing our revered system of justice can do about it?"

Case tried to maintain his composure. "Don't shoot the messenger, Les. There were things that could have been done. I understand that you believed there to be good reasons not to do those things."

Moore had been leaning against the wall, expressionless. "Stop. This is my fault. I understood the risks. I should have protected you from yourself, Les. To you it was a commune. I knew it was a business, and I should have treated it as a business. OK? So let's move on."

Werk paused, then turned and looked at Case. "Lou, whose lawyer are you. Who do you represent here?"

"As you know, for many years I've represented Owen and Moore Company. From time to time, Owen asked me to do some work for P2P Enterprises, which I did."

"Sounds like I need someone to represent me, doesn't it?"

Werk walked toward the door. Moore followed him. "What's that supposed to mean, Les?"

Werk stopped and turned around quickly, raising his voice in a way Moore had never heard. "I'm saying that I honored my part of this deal, Owen. I brought you the P2P, and I improved the hell out of it—so Guy can now make a fortune off of what I did. You were the business side. You were supposed to protect what we built. Did you honor your part?"

"Calm down, Les. There's enough blame for everyone. Let's talk solutions, not blame."

"Answer my question, Owen. *Did you honor your part of the deal?*"

Case interrupted. "Les, this is not constructive. Owen, stop right there."

Moore's thoughts drifted to the television crime shows he liked to watch. He repeated the mantra to himself. "You have the right to remain silent. Everything you say can and will be held against you . . ."

"This was all I ever had, Owen, and you blew it for me. I'm about to lose my livelihood, my life's work, my life's dream. Whose fault is that, Owen? *Whose fault?*"

Werk turned his back and walked out.

Two weeks later, Moore was served with the Complaint Werk had filed against Moore in county court. Moore faxed a copy to Case, waited fifteen minutes, and called him.

"This is hard to believe, Lou. Tell me what all this really means."

"It's not all that complicated, Owen. Werk sued you. His primary point is that you breached the agreement in which you agreed to be responsible for the business side of P2P Enterprises. He claims that if you had done what a reasonably prudent businessperson would have done, P2P would be coining money for the next decade. He says it's your fault P2P is out of business, and he wants $10 million."

"That's *nuts*. I will *not* put up with it. The P2P never would have gotten off the ground without me. I arranged for the financing. I set up the manufacturing, the marketing, the distribution—everything. What the hell else was I supposed to do?"

"I can tell you what his Complaint says you were supposed to do."

"OK, Lou, let's go through some of this."

"Werk alleges that you should have had Leavitt sign an agreement that would have protected the company if he left. Either a noncompete, or at the very least, a nondisclosure and non-solicitation agreement."

"Should I have done that?"

"Yes, Owen. I think you should have. A noncompete would have prevented Leavitt from going to work for Guy or anyone else who wanted to take your business. A nondisclosure and non-solicitation agreement isn't as good, but if they were drafted correctly, Guy might never have come after Leavitt, and even if he did, you'd have a better than even shot at staying in business."

"Those agreements really work? I've always heard you can't enforce them."

"They can work in most jurisdictions, Owen, including this one. Les's attorney has put together some other claims as well—he alleges that you could have used the trade secrets laws, the copyright laws, and the patent laws to protect the company against the kind of raid Guy has pulled off. He's got some points, Owen."

"Revisionist history! Les was the one who insisted that we operate on trust. No lawyers. No complications. It's not just about money, he'd say."

"You let that dictate how you ran the business? Come on, Owen. For lots of people it's not just about money when they first start out in business. But once they get a taste of success and the money's on the table, there to be had, it's *all* about money. You signed on to run the business, Owen. You're not going to get too far by saying that you took your cues from a guy you considered to be a business illiterate."

"All this is well and good, Lou. But the crux of the whole thing is the patent, isn't it? Les told me he had filed the patent application and all was well. I should sue Les. If he had done what he was supposed to do on the patent, the P2P would have been protected and none of my supposed failings would have mattered a damn. Guy would have been trying to buy us, not steal us."

"That's true, Owen. But let me play devil's advocate. Then you tell me how strong you think your position really is.

"First, Werk told you he filed an application, and he did. He didn't lie to you. He didn't know anything was wrong with the application. You had every opportunity to check out the prospects for his application. But you didn't. Instead, you decided to assume that all was well with a patent application filed by a nonlawyer. It's pretty doubtful that you'll be able to blame Werk for your failure to do some basic due diligence.

"Second, Werk made some serious changes to the P2P while you were working together. He came up with a more efficient solar-panel design, new power-saving circuitry, a unique battery configuration. He doubled what the P2P could do. He gave you all those details, you had the lab verify how much more efficient and cost effective they made the P2P, and you used that data in the marketing campaigns. And yet, you, the business side of this company, never made an effort to get patent protection for any of it. At the very least, the improvements could have been protected, but they weren't. Thanks to that, all Guy had to do was buy a P2P and copy it."

"So I roll over?"

"Hell, no. You've got some arguments and some leverage. We file a counterclaim, we body punch, we drag him through the mud, we run up his costs, and we try to convince Werk that his lawsuit is more trouble than it's worth. He'll use similar tactics on us."

"And . . . ?"

"I'd love to tell you it's all going to be fine, Owen. But I can't. Look, your position is more smoke than fire. Maybe Werk's lawyers won't figure that out. Ultimately, if you're lucky, we settle for something you can live with, something a lot less than what you'll probably face if you let a jury decide."

"What's it going to cost?"

"That depends on how hard they want to fight. Our job is to take the fight out of them as quickly as we can—go on the offense, let them know they're in for a world war, and hope they opt for a quick way out. But chances are it will be ugly and expensive, at least for a while. I need to go into attack mode, and I'll need a minimum $50,000 retainer."

"Good money after bad. Great."

"Then don't spend it. Light a candle. Maybe the lawsuit will go away."

Moore remained silent.

"Sorry. Look, Owen. If you got yourself into a car accident, you wouldn't blame the doctor you hired to put you back together. So don't blame me. You placed a bet, and you lost. It happens. My job is to minimize the damage. I'll do my best, but I'll need your help."

"When's this going to stop, Lou? How can I stop spending half my time and money on stuff that has nothing to do with staying in business?"

"Good question, Owen. Maybe next time you'll ask me that question *before* you make a deal instead of afterward."

■ ■ ■

## Creating the Solution—Nine Goals:
## Lots of Ammunition . . .
## but with an Expiration Date

### Before We Get Started . . .

Two foundational points need to be made before the solutions to Owen Moore's and Les Werk's travails can be reviewed.

First point: You cannot wait until a potential problem surfaces before you protect the secrets of your success—by then, it will probably be too late. This is one of those areas that demands that the protections the law provides be implemented up front, at the earliest feasible time. You'll have lots of ammunition—but it usually comes with an expiration date.

Second point: You'll need counsel. I'll repeat that message, somewhat incessantly, in the following sections. The point of this chapter is not to turn you into a do-it-yourselfer. It cannot be done. The point of this chapter is to give you the information you'll need to be an informed, responsible participant in a process that, ultimately, *must* be left in the hands of experienced professionals.

If you were building a home, you would be well advised to learn all you could about the options in roofing materials, insulation systems, heating and cooling systems, "smart home" products, and so on. If you were contemplating a medical procedure, you would want to educate yourself on the alternatives and risks. While your architect and your doctor would probably present and explain the available options, you'll want to know enough so that you can ask the right questions and meaningfully participate in the various decisions. However, as important as your participation might be, you'll still have to rely on the experts to help you make the right choices, and you'll still need someone who's been there and done that to install the geothermal system or perform the laser surgery.

Protecting the secrets of your success is a similar endeavor. My purpose, therefore, is to help you understand the threats to your existing and potential success, and how you can minimize those threats, *before* it's too late. If you can accomplish that, you will be more likely to explore your options with qualified professionals and put the protections you need into service; otherwise, you'll be more likely to suffer the consequences that so often afflict those who leap first and look later.

The most useful way to explain what you need to know is, in my view, to focus on the goals you should be trying to accomplish. Rather than trying to summarize these important concepts and principles in the abstract, we'll attempt to explain how you can use the law to get from where you are to where you need to be.

## The Goal: Preventing Key Employees from Working for the Competition

Many companies have key employees who are crucial to their success, employees their competition would love to hire. Often, they are employees with lucrative, loyal customer contacts or employees with valuable, high-level technical know-how or experienced managers who know how you do the little things that make your company successful. These employees carry with them the secrets of your success, and their loss is a double hit: it hurts you, and it helps them.

Is there anything the law can do to help you hold on to your key employees? And, conversely, is there anything in the law that would enable you to hire your competition's key employees?

As a general rule, in the right circumstances and subject to some important qualifications, you can enter into an agreement with an employee that restricts the employee's right to work for a competitor, and in so doing, you can effectively protect key business assets. But there are lots of devils in these legal details.

These agreements are often referred to as "covenants not to compete" (or "noncompete agreements," "noncompetes," or "restrictive covenants"), and your ability to utilize them will vary significantly from state to state. Some states effectively ban them—these states take the position that covenants not to compete are restraints of trade, they restrict a person's right to earn a living, and they compromise economic growth. Other states, the majority, allow covenants not to compete, but before enforcing them, courts will require that they clear a series of legal hurdles.

If you enter into an enforceable covenant not to compete with an employee, you can usually obtain an injunction precluding that employee and your competitors from violating it, and depending on how the covenant is drafted, you may also be entitled to reimbursement for the counsel fees you incur in the process.

Here are some of the key criteria that agreements of this nature must satisfy in order to be enforceable:

*The value requirement.* An employee has to receive something of substantial value (what the law calls "consideration") in exchange for agreeing to a covenant not to compete. If he doesn't, a court won't enforce it.

Agreeing to allow an existing employee to keep a job he already has so long as he signs the covenant not to compete (the "sign this, or you're fired" approach) is not sufficient. Agreeing to hire a new employee provided that he signs a covenant not to compete (the "sign this, or I will not hire you" approach) is sufficient. For that reason, you should have the employee sign the covenant not to compete *before* he begins his employment. If he starts and *then* signs, a court may find that you agreed to hire him even if he refused to sign, and that he received nothing further in exchange for the noncompete.

⋯⟶ **If you enter into an enforceable covenant not to compete with an employee, you can usually obtain an injunction precluding that employee and your competitors from violating it, and depending on how the covenant is drafted, you may also be entitled to reimbursement for the counsel fees you incur in the process.**

In the case of existing employees, other forms of substantial and meaningful consideration will generally do the trick—in most states, for instance, you can condition a significant promotion or a valuable stock option on an employee's assent to a noncompete. If the employee agrees, courts will generally find that the employee received sufficient value. Consult with counsel.

*Does the agreement serve a legitimate business interest?* Courts will only enforce a covenant not to compete to the extent required to protect the former employer's *legitimate* business interests—*legitimate* meaning that which is required to protect the former employer from real, not minor or theoretical, harm.

The court's initial focus will be on the duration of the covenant and the area it covers. Many courts will dismiss a covenant not to compete out of hand if it lacks reasonable time and geography limitations; other courts will, as they often call it, "blue pencil" the covenant—they will rewrite it so that it includes what the court feels to be a reasonable time limit and area restriction and enforce it as modified.

The question is how much time and what sort of area restriction does a former employer *really* need to protect its legitimate business interests? In the case of a salesman who built up valuable customer contacts using leads provided by his former employer, for example, a court will probably enforce an otherwise valid noncompete but only for whatever time the former employer reasonably requires to take a fair shot at establishing its own relationship with those customers—typically six months or a year, depending on the circumstances. Anything longer than that would be viewed as an attempt to punish the former employee or deter others from leaving, which in this context are not legitimate business interests.

If the covenant not to compete covered, for instance, all states east of the Mississippi, but the former employer did little business outside New England, a court would be unlikely to enforce it beyond New England—again, the larger geographic restriction would be more than what is required to protect the former employer's legitimate business interests.

Greater time limits may be permitted in the case of an employee with valuable and unique technical skills learned through his employment with the former employer. Depending on how valuable and unique the skills are, a court may conclude that it's reasonable to give the former employer a greater period to capitalize on the technologies it developed and shared before allowing a former employee to deliver them to a competitor. If the former employer only does business in part of the country, however, the former employee may be permitted to immediately take those skills to a company that does business elsewhere, since the former employer's business would not be affected if another company with which it does not compete hires the former employee.

Whether a covenant not to compete is required to protect an employer's legitimate business interests will also be analyzed from many other points of view aside from time and geography.

For instance, courts will usually refuse to enforce a covenant not to compete if the effect will be to prevent an employee from taking his own contacts and skills to a competitor. Suppose you hire a salesman who brings his own book of business with him. You sign him to a covenant not to compete, but things don't work out, and he decides to leave after just a few months. If the salesman's departure would result in little more than his taking the contacts he brought with him to a competitor, a court will probably refuse to enforce the covenant not to compete—most courts would conclude that you do not have a legitimate business interest in keeping the salesman from capitalizing on a book of business to which you did not materially contribute.

Similarly, suppose you sign a production engineer and an office manager to a covenant not to compete. They're valuable employees, but you did not give them any special training—basically, they used the education and experience they brought with them to do their jobs. Assuming you would suffer no real harm (other than the need to find their replacements) if they worked for a competitor, most courts would be reluctant to find that you have a legitimate business interest in interfering with their right to pursue career advancement.

THESE ISSUES ARE EXTREMELY fact-sensitive and are carefully reviewed on a case-by-case basis. It's best to pick your spots rather than try to impose covenants not to compete on all employees all the time—if you use noncompetes selectively, a court will be more likely to believe that you only use them when it really matters to you.

Courts will strive to analyze the *real* impact of enforcement on the former employer and will balance that against the effect enforcement will have on the former employee. If a court concludes that the harm to the employer will be minimal and the employee may not be able to find employment elsewhere, a court may refuse to enforce a covenant not to compete; if a court finds that a former employer made a real investment in a former employee who now holds the keys to the former employer's secrets of success, the covenant will likely be enforced no matter the effect enforcement may have on the former employee's job prospects. As for the cases in between, the result will depend upon the unique circumstances—among others, how long the employee was employed, the reason the employee left, the nature of the industry in question, and, sometimes most importantly, the predilections of the judge hearing the case.

The same analysis holds if you're the one seeking to recruit a valuable employee from another company. Make certain to ask the prospective employee whether he is subject to any sort of covenant not to compete (as Richard Guy asked Will Leavitt), and for your protection, have him confirm it in writing. If he has not signed a noncompete, you can recruit and hire him (except in some jurisdictions, in *extremely* unusual circumstances involving situations in which the prospective employee knows his former employer's high-level trade secrets . . . talk to counsel). If he has signed a noncompete, analyze the enforceability of the agreement with counsel and make a judgment whether the litigation risks are worth taking.

Imagine how differently events would have unfolded if Owen Moore and Les Werk had allowed Lou Case to do his job, and if Will Leavitt had been required to sign a covenant not to compete before he started with P2P Enterprises. Would it have been enforced? Everything Leavitt knew about the P2P business had been handed to him on a silver platter by Moore and Werk, and he was planning on leaving for Guy International, a company in P2P Enterprises' backyard, for the purpose of assisting Guy International's entry into a market P2P Enterprises had pioneered. In states that permit covenants not to compete, virtually all courts would prevent Leavitt from working for Guy International for a year, maybe more.

That might not have dissuaded Richard Guy—but it might have made him think about trying to buy, instead of destroy, P2P Enterprises. In addition, if the covenant not to compete had been combined with the right kinds of additional protections, discussed in the next section, Moore and Werk, not Guy, would have been spending the P2P profits.

## The Goal: Preventing Key Employees from Helping the Competition
Whether you think a covenant not to compete could help protect the secrets of your success is often a moot point: many employees simply will not sign

noncompete covenants because of the obvious effects they can have on their careers, and you'll have to decide whether you want to hire them anyway. In those cases, you should consider some alternative types of agreements that employees may find more palatable—the idea is to let them work for the competition but to limit the extent to which they can help the competition.

For example, consider a provision that for a year after termination prohibits an ex-employee who had been involved in sales from doing business with any customer with whom the ex-employee had any contact during his tenure with you. That will give you the opportunity to establish relationships with these customers free from your ex-employee's interference. Both the ex-employee and any court asked to enforce this kind of agreement will find it easier to swallow than a standard noncompete: your ex-employee won't be totally excluded from his chosen job market; he'll simply be prohibited from dealing with certain customers for a limited period. If need be, this provision can be ratcheted down a notch so that your ex-employee is only prohibited from *soliciting* those customers (though if the ex-employee does end up doing business with the customers, it may be difficult to prove whether the customers solicited him or vice versa).

> ⋯▸ **Many employees simply will not sign noncompete covenants because of the obvious effects they can have on their careers, and you'll have to decide whether you want to hire them anyway. In those cases, you should consider some alternative types of agreements that employees may find more palatable—the idea is to let them work for the competition but to limit the extent to which they can help the competition.**

In either event, make sure the provision prohibits the ex-employee from "direct or indirect" violations—as when your ex-employee feeds the name of the customer he's not allowed to contact to his new employer, and some other salesperson then contacts the customer.

If you have any information that can be reasonably considered proprietary or confidential, you should *always*, as a part of standard operating procedure, require employees to sign an agreement that prohibits them from taking, disclosing, or using those materials, or any copies or extracts from those materials, whether in hard copy or electronic formats. At the very least, this kind of agreement should carefully define the information in question, it should define what they can and cannot do with the information, and it should include clauses providing for a remedy in the case of a violation. Properly drafted, these kinds of agreements do not require time limits. This is not rocket science; any attorney with experience in this area will have been down this road many times.

As we will see, most states have laws that prohibit an employee (or anyone else) from taking information that measures up to the legal definition of a trade secret. These nondisclosure/nonuse agreements add a significant layer of protection on top of these laws—you are allowed to define what the employee is not permitted to take (whether it's a "trade secret"), you can define what happens if there's a violation, and so on. Depending on the nature of your business, this can be hugely important; you might not otherwise be able to protect, for instance, customer lists, customer purchasing histories, prospect lists, business plans, marketing plans, client presentation materials, industry studies, vendor lists, pricing information, production techniques, salary and compensation information, production costs, and profit margin information . . . all the stuff your competition would love to get its hands on.

The problem with these agreements is that it can often be difficult to find out if they have been violated. But, properly drafted and implemented, they can, at the least, provide a significant deterrent; it never hurts to provide a copy to an employee of what he signed, at an exit interview. If you find out where your former employee is working, you may also consider sending a copy of the agreement to his new employer as a warning shot across the bow—if they know their new employee agreed not to bring certain materials with him, if they know that he violated the agreement and brought the materials, and if they nevertheless accept those materials, you could have a significant claim against them.

If you are on the other side of the fence and in recruiting mode: Find out if the prospective employee has signed any sort of confidentiality agreement. If he says he has not, confirm that with him in writing; if he says he has, get a copy, and review it with counsel. If it's enforceable, you can still hire the employee, but you'll want to include provisions in your deal with him that make plain, should it become an issue later, that you instructed him to do nothing that would violate the agreement. So long as you stick by that commitment and do not knowingly participate in, or accept the benefits of, his improper conduct, that will help get you off the hook in the event the former employer claims at some later time that you hired the employee in order to obtain information you weren't entitled to receive.

Would these kinds of agreements have fended off Guy's raid on the business Moore and Werk built? At the least, it would have made Leavitt a much less valuable commodity, and it would have kept Guy from so easily learning what he needed to know to break into a market in which he had no experience. This might not have been enough by itself, but again, in combination with the other protections Moore and Werk had available to them, Guy would have had a much tougher row to hoe.

## The Goal: Increasing the Odds Key Employees Will Choose to Stay

A covenant not to compete is a stick; you can also use a carrot.

For instance, suppose you make a deal with an employee in which you agree to contribute 5 percent of the employee's base salary into an interest-bearing account on December 31 of each year during which the employee remains with your company. If the employee stays for at least ten years, he gets the money two years thereafter, provided that he does not work for a competitor in the meantime. If he leaves or is terminated for cause before the deadline, or if he violates the noncompetition provision, he forfeits the money.

These kinds of provisions, often referred to as "golden handcuffs," can substantially increase the likelihood that an employee will choose to stay—at some point, the price of leaving becomes too great. Just in case the employee does get another offer he can't refuse, however, golden handcuffs deals can be combined with noncompete agreements and, most certainly, should be combined with nondisclosure/nonuse agreements. But when the golden handcuffs work, they may make those kinds of agreements beside the point.

Golden handcuffs agreements come in limitless variations. The previous example is a simple deferred compensation arrangement. A more complicated version might be composed of an agreement in which employees can defer some part of their income into an investment account (and, at the same time, defer some taxes); the employer matches 50 percent of the deferral; if the employee stays for a certain number of years, he gets the appreciated fund, and the employer pays the deferred taxes; if not, the matched portion is returned to the employer.

> **"Golden handcuffs" can substantially increase the likelihood that an employee will choose to stay—at some point, the price of leaving becomes too great.**

Sometimes, the incentive is composed of stock options or "phantom stock" (arrangements in which employees receive profit distributions as if they own stock). Sometimes the incentive is a deferred compensation plan managed by a third party into which the employer pays premiums, or an annuity arrangement. Sometimes life insurance benefits are folded in. Financial consultants, compensation specialists, and lawyers typically work together to craft a custom-fitted arrangement.

The obvious disadvantage to a golden handcuffs deal is the expense and, depending upon the nature of the arrangement, the administration. But based on the value of the employee, the risks associated with his departure, and the cost of recruiting and replacement, it may well be worth it. Drafting the agreement the right way is also crucial—for instance, from the employee's point of view, it won't make sense if you can terminate him for no reason shortly before he would earn the benefit of the deal; from your point of view, you need to retain the right to terminate him if he's not doing his job, no matter what. Lawyers who do this kind of work know how to negotiate and solve these kinds of issues.

## The Goal: Keeping Your Independent Contractors to Yourself

Suppose you're in the restaurant supply business, and you pay a software engineering firm $100,000 to design and implement a unique, industry-specific product and customer tracking software package that helps you increase revenue by 10 percent. The next thing you know, the software engineering firm is marketing the same software package they designed for you to all other restaurant supply companies with which you compete for $10,000. Did the software engineering firm do anything wrong?

Probably not, unless you addressed the issue up front in a written agreement with the software engineering firm.

This is an important and frequently misunderstood legal reality. Companies often hire an independent contractor to create something—a computer program, a photograph, advertising copy, a logo, a marketing brochure, a product design, and so on. Even when a company hires and pays for his work, however, copyright law says that the independent contractor, *not the company*, owns the copyright to what he created. We'll cover copyright in more detail later in this chapter, but here's the point: The company will have very limited rights to what was created— it will be able to use the material for the purpose it was commissioned, and that's about it. The independent contractor, however, will have the right to do just about anything he wants with what he created, including selling copies of it to others, as often as he likes.

> ⇥ **Even when a company hires and pays for his work, however, copyright law says that the independent contractor, *not the company*, owns the copyright to what he created.**

Note that it's different in the case of a work created by an employee (as opposed to an independent contractor) as part of his employment duties—in that case, copyright law says that the employer owns the copyright. So, for instance, if a company's employee creates a computer program, a lamp design, or a magazine article as part of his job, the company owns the copyright. There are some nuances, such as making certain that the individual is really an *employee* as the term is used in the copyright law and that whatever he created was really part of his employment duties. As usual, given the complexities in this area of law, check with counsel.

You can effectively change the deal with an independent contractor, however, if you enter into the right kind of agreement *before* the independent contractor begins his work. In some circumstances, you can use what the law terms a "work made for hire" (or, sometimes, a "work for hire" or WFH) agreement: it takes the copyright from the independent contractor and automatically vests it in the person or company that hired the independent contractor. However, a WFH agreement only works in certain situations defined by copyright law. Otherwise, you can use an agreement in which the independent contractor specifically agrees to transfer all of his rights to whatever he creates to you. There are similar agreement provisions that apply to patent and other rights. These kinds of agreements require precise, specialized language; use a lawyer.

It may well be that the independent contractor will not be willing to enter into one of these agreements (or that he is willing but not at a price you're willing to pay). At least you will have identified the issue at the start, *before* the independent contractor creates the work and gets his money—and you *then* find out that he's going to resell what you thought you owned. If you confront the issues at the onset, you have some negotiating leverage—either the independent contractor agrees, or there's no deal, and you find another independent contractor. If you confront the issue at the back end, you have no leverage—the independent contractor already owns what he created, and if ownership is important to you, he can hold you up.

In addition, you may have a legitimate reason to be concerned about an independent contractor working for your competition after completing your assignment. For example, if you hire an outside controller as an independent contractor for a six-month assignment, he'll know all about your costs, your margins, your supply chain, your pay structure, and so on. If you hire a marketing consultant as an independent contractor, he will know the products you plan to introduce, the market segments you plan to pursue, your advertising strategies . . . This is the kind of information that could hurt you if it became available to your competition, and you've got a legitimate reason to try to keep that from happening.

Sometimes an independent contractor is hired to function as would a full-time employee—he does the more-or-less routine jobs typically done by full-time employees, but is paid on a different basis (which can raise other issues; talk to your lawyer or accountant). Most states that allow you to bind employees to a noncompete will allow you to bind this type of independent contractor in the same way, but there are jurisdictional differences, and the particular facts will matter, so don't automatically assume this can be done. You can also use nondisclosure/nonuse agreements in the effort to protect yourself, though, as discussed above, they don't provide the same level of security.

Companies and individuals that provide more specialized or short-term, project-specific services (such as consultants, designers, and so on) will generally be unwilling to sign a noncompete agreement that will restrict their ability to do business with a substantial segment of their market—unless your project is of sufficient size to make it worth their while, a broad noncompete will usually not make financial sense to them. But they (as well as independent contractors who work in states that do not permit noncompete agreements) generally recognize that their clients have legitimate concerns not only about the potential use and disclosure of the client's confidential or proprietary information, but also about the independent contractor's future use and resale of whatever the client paid it to create, and that often provides a foundation for a negotiated compromise.

For instance, in the earlier example, if the software engineering firm makes a good part of its living in the restaurant supply business, it probably won't be willing to stay out of that market. But you might be able to convince it not to do business with one or two identified competitors that are particularly important to you. Or, even if you are unsuccessful in obtaining a WFH or transfer of rights agreement, you might be able to convince it not to use certain portions of the code you paid it to write for any other projects. Or, perhaps, you might make a deal in which it pays you a fee for the right to use the code.

Each situation will be different, and the options will be a function of the creativity and flexibility of the parties and their lawyers. The point, however, is to foresee these issues, and confront them *before* the relationship begins. Otherwise, you may lose the opportunity to confront them at all.

## The Goal: Using Trade Secrets Law to Protect the Secrets of Your Success

Information that qualifies under the law as a *trade secret* is given specialized legal protection—those who improperly take trade secrets can be hammered for big-time damages and may even end up in jail. Whether you're trying to protect your trade secrets or are wondering about someone else's, it's crucial to understand what a trade secret is.

Almost all states have enacted a model statute called the Uniform Trade Secrets Act (UTSA). Even the states that have not adopted the act have enacted laws that are very similar to it. Here's the legal definition of *trade secret* as stated in the act:

> "Trade secret" means information, including a formula, pattern, compilation, program, device, method, technique, or process, that: (i) derives independent economic value, actual or potential, from not being generally known to, and not being readily ascertainable by proper means by, other persons who can obtain economic value from its disclosure or use, and (ii) is the subject of efforts that are reasonable under the circumstances to maintain its secrecy.

Simultaneous translation number one of trade secrets law: if the information has real business value and is not generally known to or easily discoverable by others (for instance, by consulting the industry literature or through reverse engineering), *and* you make a reasonable effort to keep it from being disclosed to those who don't need to know about it, then it's probably a trade secret. There are slight variations among states, but as a general rule and definitional niceties aside, when the law talks about a trade secret, this is what it means.

A trade secret can be a recipe for a salad dressing or the chemical formula for an industrial solvent. It can be the purchasing preferences and credit ratings of a company's customers. It can be a list of overseas suppliers of certain raw materials. It can be a computer-chip design or a computer program. It can be the format for a planned advertising campaign. It can be the manufacturing process used to create a company's key product. It can be the pay rates used for different job categories. The subjects are limitless; if it meets the definitional criteria, it's a trade secret.

Simultaneous translation number two of trade secrets law: if it's somebody else's trade secret, don't mess with it. The UTSA provides the owner of information that qualifies as a trade secret with some potent rights against anyone who takes or willingly accepts and uses the information. The owner of the information has the right to obtain an injunction requiring whoever took the information to return it, to obtain substantial damages (and even punitive damages) from whoever took it, and to recover attorneys' fees from whoever took it.

⇢ **The UTSA provides the owner of information that qualifies as a trade secret with some potent rights against anyone who takes or willingly accepts and uses the information. The owner of the information has the right to obtain an injunction requiring whoever took the information to return it, to obtain substantial damages (and even punitive damages) from whoever took it, and to recover attorneys' fees from whoever took it.**

Serious stuff. If, for example, a disgruntled employee downloads your product designs and supplier pricing information onto a flash drive and gives it to one of your competitors, and if the information qualifies as a trade secret, you will have some *very* substantial claims against all concerned.

Things became even more serious in 1996, when the federal government enacted the Economic Espionage Act (EEA). The EEA made it a crime to intentionally misappropriate or use a trade secret when doing so will harm whoever owns the trade secret. The penalty: up to ten years imprisonment and up to a $5,000,000 fine.

Civil lawsuits in which companies sue ex-employees or competitors for misappropriation of trade secrets are commonplace, and a very substantial body of law exists in this area. Most cases involve ex-employees taking materials they think will help them in their next position—such as customer lists, customer information, formulas, designs and specifications, cost and margin data, and so on. Prosecutions under the EEA occur much less frequently—but they most certainly occur. Many of these prosecutions involve employees who believe they have been treated unfairly and then try to sell sensitive information to competitors. Some involve international intrigue—selling high-tech materials to foreign governments.

The lesson is plain: if you're trying to maximize the extent to which your business information is protected, it will serve you well if that information fits within the trade secret definition; if you're attempting to obtain someone else's business information, it will serve you well to be able to distinguish that which is and is not a trade secret. The line between, for instance, lawful data mining and unlawful trade secret misappropriation is less than pristine, and a new profession has emerged from the confusion—for example, take a look at the Web site for the Society of Competitive Intelligence Professionals, at www.scip.org.

Many trade secrets are made, not born: there is a lot you can do to influence whether a court will find that your information is a trade secret. Your plan to protect the secrets of your success should, therefore, capitalize on every opportunity you have to make those secrets into trade secrets.

- Keep records on the time and expense incurred to develop the information. For example, in the case of a database of information, the more difficult and expensive it was to assemble the information, the more likely a court will be to deem it worthy of trade secret protection. The easier it is for another company to develop the same information independently, the less likely a court will protect it.

- Do you attribute internal value to the information? For example, is it shown as an asset on your balance sheet? Is it noted as something that gives your business particular value on your loan applications?

- Courts will attribute great significance to the measures you took to secure the information from those who did not need to or were not authorized to see it—a key consideration will be the extent to which you treat the information as a true secret worthy of protection. That's why Richard Guy asked Will Leavitt about the efforts P2P Enterprises took to secure its customer list. If it's in hard-copy form, is it locked away? What kind of physical security is there? Do authorized personnel have to show some form of identification to get to where the information is located, or can anyone gain access to that area? If it's in electronic form, how is it protected from access? Are there firewalls? Is the information kept on a separate server? Do computer logs reliably track who accessed the server? Have written and enforced security policies been set? Have professional security firms been used? Are background checks done on employees who might have access to the information?

- When the information is disclosed to employees or third parties, are they required to sign confidentiality and nondisclosure agreements?

Finally, it's important to remember that if you put your otherwise confidential information into the public domain, even inadvertently, it's no longer a trade secret.

For instance, if you disclose too much in a white paper presented at an industry conference or in marketing materials distributed to prospective customers, you may lose trade secret protection. Importantly, once you disclose the details in a patent application, it's public information and no longer protectable as a trade secret (and once the patent expires, it all falls into the public domain). This is why many companies choose not to file for patents and depend on trade secrets law instead—for instance, the vaunted Coca-Cola formula has never been patented. If the secret method you use to create a product can be reverse engineered from the product itself, it's not a trade secret (in which case seeking a patent may be the best alternative).

In exceptional cases, other types of protection can serve the same purpose. For example, there are those who claim to have chemically deciphered the Coca-Cola recipe. But the Coke formula and flavor may also be subject to trademark protection, making efforts to capitalize on the purported discovery a risky proposition . . . more about that later. And there's a practical aspect to all of this as well: right or wrong, there aren't many companies willing or able to withstand the litigation onslaught that would result if they claimed to be selling duplicate Coke. Might does not always make right, but sometimes it's the functional equivalent.

## The Goal: Using Copyright Law to Protect the Secrets of Your Success

How can you obtain a copyright on your secrets of success? How might a copyright help you protect those secrets? Here's the general idea:

Whoever creates what the copyright law calls an "original work of authorship," which covers virtually any form of expression that includes an element of originality, owns the copyright in that work (except, as explained previously, in the case of employees who create works for their employers—in those cases, the employer owns the copyright). To be subject to copyright protection, the work has to be in a tangible form—on paper, on the Internet, on tape or film, on a hard drive, embodied in a product, and so on.

A copyrighted work can be literary and artistic (a novel, a painting, a film, a song), but it doesn't have to be. Copyright law also applies to the crass and commercial work product that businesses routinely generate: a manufacturing-procedure manual, an engineering or architectural plan, a formula for a chemical compound, a marketing brochure, a contract clause, an inventory-tracking form, a computer program, a PowerPoint presentation, an instructional video, a series of product photographs, a fabric pattern . . .

Once you own the copyright on a work, you own the exclusive right to reproduce and sell that work, you can stop others from creating spin-offs based on what you've created, and, importantly, you can sell or license those rights to others as you see fit.

> **···⟩ For most businesses, copyright law provides little meaningful protection. It is dangerous to mistake copyright protection for something it's not.**

What does all this boil down to in the real world? On the surface, it seems that copyright law can be quite useful in protecting the secrets of your success. However, in fact, for most businesses, copyright law provides little meaningful protection. It is dangerous to mistake copyright protection for something it's not.

Here is the chink—actually, the gaping hole—in the copyright law's armor: Copyright law only protects the *form* in which an idea or concept is expressed, *not* the idea or concept itself. Trade secrets law and patent law can protect your idea or concept; copyright law cannot.

Let's suppose you come up with a revolutionary idea on how to make computer chips function more efficiently. You create a detailed white paper that explains the process, and you register the copyright on the white paper with the Copyright Office in Washington, D.C. You use your breakthrough as a marketing tool. You provide copies of the white paper to existing and prospective customers and tell them that you originated this copyrighted process and own the exclusive rights to use it.

A few months later, you find out that several competitors are using *your* idea, and basing *their* marketing campaigns on it. What now? It's your idea, and it's copyrighted. Can they do that?

They can. Copyright law does *not* protect your chip-manufacturing breakthrough. Your competitors are free to use it as they wish. At most, copyright law only protects the words you chose to explain your breakthrough in your white paper. And even in that context, while copyright law prohibits your competitors from using substantially similar words, it does not prevent them from using different words to explain the very same ideas.

Suppose you run a restaurant. You come up with several new and creative entrées and give them each a snappy name. Your dishes are wildly popular, so you decide to publish the recipes in a copyrighted cookbook. Shortly thereafter, two neighboring restaurants begin serving the very same dishes under different names. Can you stop them? No, your copyright only protects how you described the recipes, not the recipes themselves.

In 1979, when the personal computer market was in its earliest stages, two programmers introduced the first electronic spreadsheet, VisiCalc. As the personal computer market grew, VisiCalc sold well, more than 700,000 copies—and in the process it attracted the competitors that ultimately put it out of business. VisiCalc had been copyrighted, but not patented; it was not clear at the time that computer programs were patentable. Because the copyright only protected how the VisiCalc program was expressed (and not the idea of a spreadsheet program), competitors could easily duplicate what VisiCalc did so long as they did not substantially duplicate the program code and program appearance. VisiCalc's copyright was, essentially, worthless.

Copyrights are equally useless in protecting the kinds of things you might use to market your business, such as titles, short phrases, slogans, and familiar symbols or designs. Trademark law, discussed later, might be of help in that vein.

Copyright law is crucial for certain businesses that deal in the kinds of products that can be protected by copyright. Publishers who sell books or forms will depend on the protections the copyright law provides to them. So will movie and music distributors. So will companies that sell products with original designs they do not want duplicated—for example, apparel, furniture, homes. But for most businesses most of the time, copyright provides little more than a false sense of security. When the focus is on protecting the ideas, the methods, and the know-how that makes a company successful, copyright law provides little help.

On the other side of the coin, be careful about copying works (not only written works but, for example, designs) created by others. Copyright infringement claims can be very expensive and very ugly.

Many people believe if something does not contain a copyright notice or the familiar © symbol, it's fair game. Many people also believe that a copyright is not valid unless it's been registered with the Copyright Office. Not true—copyright protection attaches as soon as the work is put into a tangible form. There are substantial benefits to be obtained by placement of the copyright notice and through registration (for example, you cannot file a copyright infringement lawsuit if you have not registered the copyright), but the existence of the copyright itself does not depend on them.

Many people believe that if it's on the Internet, it's in the public domain and up for grabs. Not true—the mere fact that materials are published on the Internet does not diminish the author's copyright.

Many people believe that if they give credit when they use something created by someone else, that gets them off the hook. Not true—the improper use of another person's work is copyright infringement, even if you give credit.

There are, however, many ways you can copy or quote a work that has been copyrighted by someone else. It may be that what you want to copy or quote has become part of the public domain and is no longer protected by copyright law. It may be that you will have the right to do what you want under the doctrine of "fair use"—a vague (and, therefore, dangerous and frequently litigated) provision in the copyright law that allows one to use another's copyrighted work for purposes of criticism, comment, news reporting, teaching, scholarship, or research.

It will all depend on the specifics of the situation. Courts look at context—what's permissible for a scholarly, noncommercial purpose might not be permissible if the copied materials are used to generate profits. Courts look at whether the copied portions duplicate the central "essence" of the original work or merely take excerpts. They look at whether the copying will diminish the prospective sales of the original work. Courts will want to know how much of the original work was copied or quoted—just a couple snippets from a much larger work or five pages from a ten-page article? They look at what was done with the copied material—was it just used on a temporary basis, or was it incorporated in something else and republished? Check with counsel.

## The Goal: Using Trademark Law to Protect the Secrets of Your Success

For some businesses, the secret of their success lies in their brand—they've developed a favorable reputation that's associated with the name and logo they use to market a product or service. Maybe the reputation is based on reliability; maybe it's low cost; maybe it's innovation; maybe it's prestige. In the same way that some computer aficionados want only "Macs," some barbecue devotees want only "Webers," and some people favor Nike apparel that has the "swoosh" logo, the name and/or symbols associated with the product or service they sell matters, and it matters a great deal, whether in the consumer or the business-to-business arena.

And then they blow it. They don't protect the recognition and reputation they have so carefully cultivated.

The core purpose of trademark law is to protect buyers from confusion respecting the source and quality of what they are buying. When a consumer stops at a restaurant with golden arches, he's being told that he's going to get a McDonald's hamburger; when he buys a container that says "Tropicana," he's being told who supplied what he's about to drink; when he pulls into a "Jiffy Lube," he's got an expectation of the services he can buy there; when he sees the stylized "IBM" letters or the "Johnson & Johnson" name, he knows who's standing behind what he's buying. Trademark law is designed to assure the accuracy of the information being conveyed about a product or service associated with certain names and symbols—its purpose is to assure that we're dealing with whom we think we're dealing with, and we're getting what we think we're getting.

But trademark law does not stop there: it can also protect the names, symbols, and other distinctive criteria that companies use to brand themselves and their products. If, recalling a prior example, you form DooMorDad Inc. and spend $1 million to successfully develop and market the DooMorDad product, you want to make sure that others cannot thereafter ride in on your coattails and market their own DooMorDads, or, for that matter, DoMoreDads or DuMorDads or do business under those names. In addition to misleading consumers, they'll be capitalizing on your efforts and taking money out of your pocket. And if their products are of a lesser quality, something you can't control, they'll ruin the reputation you struggled to build and make it more difficult for you to do business in the future. You can use trademark law to keep and protect what you've built.

⋯⋯⟶ **Trademark law is designed to assure the accuracy of the information being conveyed about a product or service associated with certain names and symbols—its purpose is to assure that we're dealing with whom we think we're dealing with, and we're getting what we think we're getting. But trademark law does not stop there: it can also protect the names, symbols, and other distinctive criteria that companies use to brand themselves and their products.**

This is, yet again, another "don't try this at home" topic. Trademark law, like copyright law, and to an even greater extent patent law (discussed in the next section), is layered, multifaceted, and replete with subtle policy and philosophical distinctions. There are some excellent books on the market that explain the procedures and nuances of trademark law (as well as copyright and patent law), but they can only take you so far. Even experienced commercial lawyers rely on intellectual property law specialists to guide them around the hazards that only those who do intellectual property law for a living will know are there.

But you can, literally, profit from trademark law if all you know is this: trademark law exists, and if securing and preserving your name and brand is important to your business, talk to someone who knows these ropes.

Owen Moore and Les Werk pioneered the concept of a portable, renewable, home-energy source that came to be known as the P2P—as the first to enter the field, the term *P2P* became the name of not only their product, but also the concept, which made it an extremely valuable and, if need be, salable asset. Richard Guy, a prospective competitor, wanted to know, right up front, whether Moore and Werk had done anything to protect the P2P name and was most pleased to find out that they had not.

Why didn't Moore and Werk opt to protect the brand name they built? They had no experience in the world of trademarks, and they resisted Lou Case's effort to (as they saw it) complicate their business. Perhaps they did not realize that the P2P name was something that *could* be protected. They could not choose an option without knowing the option was there for the choosing.

There are some basics you should know that will make you a more intelligent and participatory consumer of trademark law services. Take these as "heads-up" points only; there is much, much more to know.

*Choosing the trademark.* Selecting the words and symbols that will comprise your trademark is a crucial decision. Obviously, you'll want something that serves your marketing purposes, something that customers will ultimately recognize as referring to what you sell. But there are important legal criteria to consider as well.

So-called descriptive marks that focus on a feature or quality of your product or service will be hard to protect under the trademark law because they don't clearly point to who's behind the product. For instance, *Springfield Software* is not sufficiently unique—there could be lots of software developers in Springfield and choosing this name would not clearly indicate to consumers the source of the software. For similar reasons, Miller was not permitted to trademark the word *lite* in conjunction with its beer. There are lots of "lite" or "light" beers, and the word *lite* doesn't clearly indicate which beer company is behind the lite beer being offered for sale.

So-called suggestive marks are easier to protect but still problematic. A suggestive mark suggests something about the product but includes some imaginative elements that make it more than merely descriptive. For instance, *Rent-a-Wreck* suggests the kind of cars you're likely to rent, *Coppertone* suggest the suntanning results you're likely to achieve, and *Roach Motel* suggests where the roaches in your home will end their lives.

The easiest mark to protect is what the law calls an "arbitrary" or "fanciful" mark—these are terms that have the least likelihood of confusion, because by their nature they don't link to the same type of product sold by some other company. These can be words not normally associated with the product (Delta Airlines, Snickers, Radio Shack) or invented words (Exxon, Rolex, Google, Microsoft).

The fact that a mark is easier to protect under the law does not necessarily mean that it's the best mark for your product or service—you may want to use a mark that describes your product, even just a little bit, and risk some additional legal fees for the purpose of ultimately getting the mark approved.

*It can be more than just a name.* In the right circumstances, you can trademark a logo, a slogan, the shape and color of the container your product comes in, how your stores are decorated, a sound, a tune . . . almost anything that can be used to build a link between your products and services and your customers. Perfume companies often trademark the shapes of the bottles they use. UPS has protected the shade of brown it uses, and Kodak has done the same for its characteristic yellow packaging. "It's the Real Thing," "Tastes Great, Less Filling," "Got Milk?"—all trademarked.

*Business names are not necessarily trademarks.* The fact that you've registered the name of your company in the states where you do business does *not* protect it in other states. Other companies in other states could use your company name. If, however, you trademarked your company name, you would be entitled to a much higher level of protection.

Businesses cannot trademark their names unless they use them in conjunction with the products and services they market—remember, the point of trademark law is to prevent consumers from being confused about the source of a product or service. So, if ABC Company markets its products and services under the DooMorDad name, the ABC Company name, not being directly associated with a product or service, cannot be trademarked. But if DooMorDad Inc. markets the DooMorDad product, its name might be subject to trademark protection, in the same way that Coca-Cola and Google, whose corporate names are the same as their products or services, are trademarked.

*Who used it first?* One of the keys to choosing a trademark is, obviously, determining if it's legally available, which can be much, much more difficult than it might seem.

The government runs the United States Patent and Trademark Office (USPTO) in Washington, D.C. Many businesspeople reasonably believe that the first person to register a trademark with the USPTO has the right to that trademark. It's not so. In the United States (unlike most of the rest of the world), it is a trademark's *use*, not registration, that matters: whoever first *uses* the trademark in a particular market receives the exclusive rights to the trademark in that market, whether or not it's registered.

A typical scenario might involve a business in Pennsylvania that comes up with a trademark, achieves success, and wants to expand nationally. So it accesses the USPTO's Web site (www.uspto.gov), uses its excellent trademark search engine, verifies that no one else has claimed the trademark, registers the trademark, and embarks on a national advertising campaign. Shortly thereafter, it is hammered with three lawsuits in three different states brought by three companies that had been using the trademark in their market, without registering it, for several years—each of which it will likely lose.

Trademark lawyers know how to conduct a full search (and, even then, there are no guarantees) and how to protect a trademark and minimize the risk of infringements. The registration process can be daunting and complicated, depending on the mark you've chosen and whether similar marks are in existence.

*And* . . . There's a lot more to know. A lot. What about Internet domain names? If you use a trademark in conjunction with shoes, can someone else use the same trademark in conjunction with tires? What about protecting your trademark overseas? Do you have to file a lawsuit if someone is infringing on your trademark? How close does someone have to come to a trademark before it constitutes infringement? How can you most effectively license others to use your trademark? Is there a way to combine copyright and trademark protection? How can you build the value of your trademark so you can eventually sell it? Use a lawyer with experience in this field.

## The Goal: Using Patent Law to Protect the Secrets of Your Success

A patent gives you the right to prevent your competition from making, using, or selling that which is patented. A patent can be a supremely effective way to protect and maximize the value of your secrets of success. If Les Werk had consulted patent counsel and handled the patent process correctly, he and Owen Moore would be spending lots of Richard Guy's money.

Patent law, however, is not for do-it-yourselfers like Les Werk. Patent law lends itself to do-it-yourselfers about as much as open-heart surgery and space shuttle launches.

The patent process abounds with technical requirements at every turn. For example, Les Werk didn't know that according to patent law he had only one year to file for a patent after describing his invention in a publication, and his ignorance became Richard Guy's bliss. Whether it's better to file for a patent (which lasts only twenty years) or rely on trade secrets law protection (particularly if the invention cannot be reverse engineered) is a question worthy of careful analysis. How to frame a patent application for maximum effectiveness, and how to prosecute it after it's filed, depends on a variety of arcane and strategic considerations that require specialized experience and expertise to disentangle. And on top of everything else—and there is ton of everything else to know—patent law is changing at a rapid pace, as both the courts and Congress confront the collision among existing patent concepts, modern technologies, and the greater social good.

As is the case with trademark law, the most valuable advice any book can give to businesses whose secrets of success may involve patentable inventions is this: patent law is probably not what you think it is; you should not even think about attempting to protect your patent rights without the advice of patent counsel; and if you delay, you might lose whatever rights you would have been able to secure. In my experience, most businesspeople generally understand these realities, but often, they wait too long to seek the advice of patent counsel. In the patent world, timing can be everything.

Werk's life would have changed if he knew about the simple rule that ended up invalidating the P2P patent application, and there are similar rules. For instance, some businesses won't even begin to think about incurring the expense associated with a patent application until they've offered their invention to customers and determined if there is a market for it. Or they'll show it at a trade show and gauge the extent of the interest. That can be deadly: you've got one year from the date you do that to get a U.S. patent, and if you show your new product before you file for an international patent, you'll lose your international patent rights.

> ⇢ **As is the case with trademark law, the most valuable advice any book can give to businesses whose secrets of success may involve patentable inventions is this: patent law is probably not what you think it is; you should not even think about attempting to protect your patent rights without the advice of patent counsel; and if you delay, you might lose whatever rights you would have been able to secure.**

Suppose that Werk (or, for that matter, anyone else) had published an article describing, even generally, the energy-storage system that was ultimately incorporated into the P2P before the P2P patent application was filed. If the article was published more than a year before the U.S. patent application was filed, the energy-storage system could not be included in the U.S. patent. International patents are not so forgiving—*anything* in print before an international patent application is filed will be excluded from the patent.

Unlike trademark law, in which first use is more important than first filing, an invention is not protected until a patent is issued by the USPTO—until then, it's basically a free-for-all. Moreover, delay holds the door open for someone else to file first, and even an obliquely related filing can seriously compromise your rights.

For these and a host of other reasons, if you've concluded (after consultation with counsel) that patent protection will work to your advantage, file as soon as possible. You don't have to have everything figured out when you file—protect what you can as soon as you can. You can amend or file additional applications later when and if your invention evolves.

There's a second, more insidious problem that keeps businesspeople from obtaining the patent advice they require: they don't realize that they may be sitting on something worthy of patent protection. They understand that if they invent a device, in the sense of a machine or even a household gadget, they should seek a patent. But they don't understand how patent law can protect their *other* secrets of success, and as a result, they fail to capture the true value of what they have created. For instance . . .

*Patenting "processes."* The Patent Act says that you can obtain a patent on the following: "any new and useful process, machine, manufacture, or composition of matter, or any new and useful improvement thereof." Note the use of the word *process*. You can patent more than just machines and devices; you can patent the way that you accomplish something, your new and better way of getting something done.

To be patentable, any invention, including a process, has to meet certain legal criteria: it has to be "novel," which basically means that there are no similar inventions; it has to be "nonobvious," which basically means that it would not be automatically apparent to someone who is skilled in the field, but rather, it results from genuine creativity; and it has to be "useful," in that it must achieve a stated purpose.

Businesses develop processes that meet these standards all the time, and some of them have potentially broad-based value. Typical patentable processes would include a new way to create an industrial compound or to clean an industrial effluent or to increase the life of a conveyor belt or to dissipate the heat in an office building or to assemble the components in a piece of equipment or to increase the durability of certain textiles or . . . You get the point. If you can patent a process that has a potential market, you can, for instance, prevent others from using it without your permission, and you can market and license it to other companies for a royalty.

*Business method patents.* For many years, the USPTO took the position that "methods of doing business" were not patentable processes. Nevertheless, in 1997, Amazon.com filed a patent application on its "1-click" ordering system—a now-familiar Internet ordering protocol in which a customer enters his address, credit card, and other data once, the system saves the data, and on future visits the customer can order with just one mouse click and avoid the need to reenter the data. Referencing the Patent Act, Amazon's position was that its 1-click method of doing business was a process, it was novel, it was nonobvious, and it was useful.

To the surprise of many, the USPTO granted the patent in 1999. This allowed Amazon to file patent infringement lawsuits and, ultimately, to make lucrative patent licensing deals with others who wanted to use a 1-click system, such as Apple. Around the same time, a federal court also ruled that a "method of doing business" *was* patentable—the case involved a computerized method to determine mutual fund pricing. A firestorm of criticism resulted—if these business methods could be patented, what else could be patented? Had patent protection gone too far?

A flood of so-called business method patent applications followed—many of which were granted—on ostensibly new ways to do business involving, for example, e-commerce, achieving tax savings, processing documents, and so on. The obvious incentive for obtaining a business method patent was the potential to force other companies who might be unwittingly utilizing a similar business method to pay substantial damages and license fees.

Things quickly got out of hand. For example, the USPTO issued patents for a janitorial-training system, a female-undergarment-sizing method, a method for exercising a cat using a laser pointer, and a method for holding a golf club when putting.

In the face of a growing backlash, the USPTO invalidated certain aspects of the Amazon patent in 2007, and later issued new guidelines. In 2008, an influential federal court ruled that business method patents should be reined in. However, the effect of these rulings has been to confuse, rather than clarify, the subject—they raise as many questions as they answer, and the battle continues. Almost inevitably, the Supreme Court will have to take on the issue and define the boundaries.

For now, however, business methods *can* be patented (although, it seems, not as easily as when Amazon filed its application), and if you have developed a truly novel and useful business method, consider it. Patent counsel will be able to advise you on the USPTO's current position and the latest court rulings.

*Design patents.* Most businesses do not know that they can patent the design of an object based solely on its aesthetic qualities, having nothing to do with how it works or what it does.

As with other patents, the design has to be novel and nonobvious, and in addition, it must have "ornamental" features that set it apart. For instance, the unique shape of a wineglass or computer monitor, a fabric pattern, the appearance features of a cell phone, the silhouette of a dress . . . they are all potentially patentable, based solely on the way they look, if they meet the criteria.

You can also copyright a design, though the protection afforded by design patents is much broader (but more difficult and expensive to obtain).

*Computer programs.* As mentioned previously, you can copyright a computer program. However, copyright protection only prohibits copying the program itself in the sense of duplicating the code and appearance of the program. Patent protection, which became available thanks to a 1981 Supreme Court decision, is much more comprehensive and valuable. It not only prohibits copying, it also prohibits others from developing programs that do essentially the same thing as the patented program—a type of protection that would have made the VisiCalc developers extremely wealthy. If your business has developed a program that produces a result in a new and better way, it may be a patentable and potential secret of success.

## The Goal: Using NDAs to Secure the Secrets of Your Success

Here's the usual scenario. You've got a novel idea or you have developed a new product—maybe it's a more efficient food-processing concept, maybe it's a better way to make automobile braking systems, maybe it's a new pension plan model. You're at the point at which you need a financial backer to fully capitalize on what you've created. Or, perhaps, you want to discuss a potential joint venture or distribution deal with an established player in your market.

In the process of discussing what you need, you'll obviously have to disclose the details of your idea or product—and that can trigger a series of problems.

The most obvious risk is that your idea or product will be stolen by the people you disclose it to, and to prevent that from happening, many individuals and companies routinely use a nondisclosure agreement (NDA). Before any disclosures are made, the recipient of the information is required to sign the NDA—at its core, the NDA will precisely describe what is being disclosed, it will limit the purpose for which the disclosures may be used, it will prohibit any further disclosures, and it will provide for certain rights and remedies in the event of a violation.

Nondisclosure agreements can serve a very useful purpose, but they are far from a panacea, and they sometimes foster a false sense of security. For example, if your idea is patentable, disclosure, with or without an NDA, might invalidate future international patent applications and could start the one-year period within which you must file a U.S. patent application. Certain types of disclosures, even with an NDA in place, might also invalidate trade secret protections.

> ⇢ **Nondisclosure agreements can serve a very useful purpose, but they are far from a panacea, and they sometimes foster a false sense of security.**

Many companies will not sign an NDA—in which event you will either have to take your chances or rely on copyright or patent protection (depending on the nature of what you're disclosing). Many companies will sign an NDA, but they'll insist on using a form with holes that might not be evident to the uninitiated. For instance, NDA forms often include a provision that allows the company to which you disclose an idea to use it if the company already had the idea in development or if the company subsequently obtains information about a similar idea from another source. Unethical companies will then steal your idea based on the phony claim that they already knew about it or were later told about it by someone else—leaving you with little but a David vs. Goliath lawsuit.

The message: protecting the secrets of your success is never as easy as you'd like it to be.

It is essential to keep in mind that the assortment of options available to protect the secrets of your success operate with different degrees of effectiveness based on what you are trying to protect, the nature of the competition, and the specific circumstances you face. A customer list compiled by a company that deals in generic commodities for which a wide range of buyers is available has limited value to the company's competitors; a customer list compiled by a company that makes specialized products for which a limited number of buyers exists is extremely valuable to the customer's competitors and merits a different and more robust protective plan involving a combination of techniques. Some employees possess the kind of knowledge and customer contacts that demand covenants not to compete; with others, a simple confidentiality agreement will more than suffice. The lifeblood of some companies is composed of highly valued and technical processes and products; for others, it's the appearance and design of their goods; for still others, it's the computer programs they use to provide their consulting services. What works in one context will not work in another.

In each case, the task is to review the menu of alternatives, assess their pros and cons, measure their costs and benefits, and develop an integrated, interwoven, targeted strategy. There is no one way, and there are no assurances of success. There is only the best you can do; make certain that you bring your best efforts, your best judgment, and your best advisors to the planning and decision-making process. It's that important.

CHAPTER FOUR

# The Fourth Mistake: Climbing Mountains that Should Have Been Molehills, Fighting Battles that Don't Have to Be Fought

EVERY COMPANY DEALS WITH PROBLEMS that consume time and resources. But there is a distinction between most companies and truly successful companies: the former seem to be continually mired in problems; the latter deal with them much less frequently, and those that they do face are generally of lesser intensity.

That's a distinction that makes a real difference—successful companies spend less time and resources *fixing* their business and more time and resources *building* their business. How do they do it? What accounts for the difference?

Part of it, of course, results from the fact that some companies have an intrinsically better business model, and some businesspeople make better decisions than others. Apart from that, there's something else: successful companies make a disciplined and strategic commitment to step away from the here and now, look into the future, identify the most significant problems that are likely to surface, and preempt them, or at least minimize them, before they ripen into crises. This abates not only the frequency, but also the severity, of the distractions and dysfunctions that rob companies of their growth potential. Accidents waiting to happen are stopped before they start. Would-be disasters become manageable nuisances. Latent lawsuits turn into minor skirmishes.

Less successful companies, on the other hand, rarely move beyond the relentless pressures of the moment. They respond to what business life throws at them as and when it happens—the "Whac-a-Mole" management model. It's human nature. We naturally focus on the problems that stare us in the face, not on the potential problems that, after all, are off in the future and may never come to fruition. We cross bridges when we get to them.

This approach creates a self-perpetuating downward spiral that feeds on itself: the less time spent on preventing problems, the more problems there are; the more problems there are, the less time there is to spend preventing problems . . . and so the cycle goes. The upshot is that less successful companies spend time and resources climbing mountains that should have been molehills. They end up fighting battles that did not have to be fought. Too much of their creativity, energy, and money are spent on the avoidance of losses, instead of the pursuit of gains.

## Understanding the Problem:
## Obvious Issues, Hidden Solutions

To businesses trying to escape from these doldrums, the law is both a culprit and a cure.

The law is a culprit because it inspires so many of the issues and complications that can suck a business dry—and in important respects, we should be grateful that it does. Our legal system is structured so that everyone gets access to the courthouse to seek justice as they see fit: we have a vast assortment of rights, we are free to pursue them as we like, and there is, thank goodness, no pre-screening by some all-powerful authority. Moreover, when a claim is made, our system provides the defendant with an arsenal of defenses and a series of opportunities to state his case, all intended, thank goodness, to safeguard against a rush to judgment. This inevitably opens the door for abuse, and it makes the process maddeningly plodding and procedural. A democratic system of justice has its price, both for a plaintiff (whose valid claim can be delayed and financially depleted into oblivion) and for a defendant (for whom the price of defeating a bogus claim can be Pyrrhic, at best).

The law is a cure in the sense that, in response to the inherent systemic failings in our laws and legal system, it has enabled a battery of tried-and-true business tactics and methods that can eliminate, reduce in frequency, or diminish the severity of these wasteful and often pointless issues and complications. The clashes between competing business interests do not always have to be so unjust, illogical, and expensive. There *are* solutions.

**→ The law is a cure in the sense that, in response to the inherent systemic failings in our laws and legal system, it has enabled a battery of tried-and-true business tactics and methods that can eliminate, reduce in frequency, or diminish the severity of these wasteful and often pointless issues and complications.**

But there's a catch, a disconnect that makes it difficult for businesses to link these law-inspired problems with their law-enabled solutions: While the problems the law fosters are all too obvious, the solutions the law facilitates are often unknown or incomprehensibly arcane; consequently the problems thrive, unchallenged by the available solutions. Among companies committed to forward-thinking management, this is the impediment that most often stands in their way.

The result is a seemingly unflagging flow of issues and disputes involving customers, vendors, consultants, investors, partners—the everyday grist for the business mill. Sometimes, these problems can have a devastating potential. More often, they are not, taken individually, life-threatening, but cumulatively and over time they can suffocate a business, keeping it constantly focused on all the wrong things, killing it with a thousand legal cuts.

In this chapter, we explore the connections between these law-inspired issues and their law-enabled solutions—the crucial pathways that do not appear on the business GPS by which most companies navigate.

# Creating the Solution: The Legal Toolbox

The solutions to many of these problems are found in a kind of "legal toolbox." The toolbox houses some largely unknown, underutilized, and ingenious tactics that can help you outflank, if not altogether elude, the most common consumers of time and money. I frequently hear owners and executives talk about certain issues and complications as "a risk of doing business," as if they are inevitable and unavoidable. Some of them are; most are not. The task, from my perspective, is to educate companies about the legal toolbox, and to show them what tools are in it and how they can be used. If I can do that, I can usually help a company make the important transition from a reactive to a preemptive approach to the issues they face.

## Preliminary Point Number One: The Contract Rule Book

···} **In business, one of the most challenging games of strategy, the rules are largely based on principles of contract law, and the legal toolbox is composed of methods and maneuvers that allow you to use contract law both offensively and defensively, as a sword and a shield.**

You cannot win a game based on strategy—chess, poker, baseball—without an intimate knowledge of the rules and without knowing how to use (and, sometimes, manipulate) the rules to your advantage. In business, one of the most challenging games of strategy, the rules are largely based on principles of contract law, and the legal toolbox is composed of methods and maneuvers that allow you to use contract law both offensively and defensively, as a sword and a shield.

You will need to understand three important concepts in order to obtain the leverage that contract law—in combination with the legal toolbox—provides.

*How contracts are formed.* At their root, most contracts involve a communication that can be fairly interpreted as an offer to buy or sell something, met by an unconditional acceptance of the offer.

It is important to realize that for purposes of forming contracts, informal, colloquial language works just as well as arcane "legalese." "I'll give you $1,000 for that widget" is an offer to buy. "I'd take $1,000 for my widget" is an offer to sell. Similarly, everything from "OK" to "It's a deal" is an acceptance. No magic words, no whereases and wherefores are needed. A ten-second conversation or a casual exchange of one-line e-mails can result in a contract that is as legally enforceable as any ever made.

At the moment language that can be interpreted as an offer is met by language that can be interpreted as an acceptance, a contract comes into being with the full force of the law behind it.

*How contracts are not formed.* If the response to an offer does not agree with *all* of the terms of the offer, it is a rejection, not an acceptance, and no contract is formed. This is often called the mirror image rule—in order to be an acceptance, the response must be the mirror image of the offer.

Sounds simple, but rejections can be complex creatures. Consider this response to an offer to purchase a piece of machinery for a stated price: "OK, so long as I can deliver in thirty days." Acceptance or rejection? Despite the *OK*, a court would likely view that in two ways. First, it's a rejection—rather than being the mirror image of the offer, the purported acceptance was conditioned on an agreed delivery date. Second, it's a counteroffer to sell the machinery with the added delivery term. In response, the buyer could accept or reject, or communicate his own counteroffer, and the contract dance would continue until (if ever) an offer is met with mirror image acceptance.

Suppose the response was as follows: "OK, it's a deal. But I'd like to deliver in thirty days." Acceptance or rejection? A court may well view that as an acceptance, even if that's not how it was intended—the offer was accepted unconditionally, and the added language was a request made after the deal was already done.

What you say, not what you *meant* to say, is what matters in contract law. If you want to reject an offer, reject it plainly. You can couple it with a counteroffer so long as you make your rejection clear. Don't make a court parse the difference between "I accept, but only if . . ." and "I accept, and I'd also like . . ." Instead, make it unequivocal, as in "I reject that offer, but I would make the deal if . . ."

*Contract mythology.* There are some myths about contracts that consistently get businesses into trouble. We alluded to some of these in earlier chapters, but they are worth highlighting.

First, oral contracts are, in almost all contexts, as legally enforceable as written contracts. There are only a very few circumstances in which a writing is required. The problem with an oral contract is, of course, the inevitable disagreements about what was really agreed to (read: the "my word against your word" issue).

Second, what the parties call their transaction doesn't matter. Many businesspeople will protest that whatever happened was only "a handshake deal" or "an agreement in principle" or "a letter of intent." It's all about what you said and did in the offer-acceptance process, not what you named what you said and did.

Third, "I never intended to make a contract" is generally not an excuse. Again, it's what you said and did—what the law books call your "objective manifestations of assent"—that matters. If a reasonable, neutral observer would interpret what you said as an unequivocal offer and the other side accepts it or would view your response to an offer as an unequivocal acceptance, you have yourself a contract, like it or not.

## Preliminary Point Number Two: Don't Try This at Home

The same message as in the previous two chapters, different context . . .

What I've told you about contract law, and what I'm about to tell you about the contract law–based techniques in the legal toolbox, will help you a great deal. However, you also need to know that contract law is a challenging, complex, and nuanced field, so let's be clear: while I can give you a broadly applicable foundation that will, indeed, help you convert mountains into molehills and wars into squabbles, I cannot equip you with everything you need to know in order to correctly and effectively use these approaches in each of the contexts to which they will be applicable. To do that, you *will* need the help of competent counsel. Think of it this way: you can download a map showing the most popular paths used to climb Mount Everest, but that doesn't mean you'll be able to make it through all the hazards and contingencies you'll confront during the trip. You'll still need the help of a professional guide at each stage along the way.

Depending on the nature of your business, you might require no more than an initial analysis so that your lawyer can become familiar with how you do business, followed by some simple document drafting and basic guidelines. That, combined with the kind of Attorney Hotline relationship we discussed in Chapter One, might well be all you need. Others, however, will require more than that, maybe much more than that.

This is not a commercial for lawyers: on the contrary, your lawyer will make more money from your travails if you eschew attempts to prevent problems and let things get out of hand. My point is that the concepts in the legal toolbox are not off-the-shelf plug-ins; they will usually take some customization and judgment by an attorney who is experienced in the representation of businesses and businesspeople. My goal has been to attune you to the fact that these approaches exist, since you are more likely to gainfully pursue a solution if you know that there is a solution to be pursued. But you can't always do this properly (or safely) by yourself.

So, to be blunt, in order to take advantage of the legal toolbox, you'll have to spend some money. If you don't, you will pay a steeper price later on. Decades ago, there was a popular commercial featuring a mechanic selling an oil filter. "You can pay me now," he'd leer, holding up the filter, "or you can pay me later," referring to the expensive engine job you'd need unless you spent a few dollars on his product.

Lawyers (and dentists, doctors, roofing contractors, accountants, plumbers . . .) live in that same world. You can spend a little bit now so that you can understand and implement the available preventive measures the right way, or you can take a pass, and spend a whole lot more later on.

## Getting Paid: Making Yourself More Trouble Than You're Worth

The most basic tools in the legal toolbox help to get you paid.

Many businesspeople do the right thing, just because it's right. Many others, unfortunately, only do the right thing if they can't get away with doing the wrong thing. They do what is in their self-interest and no more. If they don't need your goodwill, and if they figure you won't come after them or you'll severely compromise the debt to avoid an expensive lawsuit, the likelihood of a financial beating increases accordingly. As a result, too many companies spend too much time and too many resources trying to collect what they're owed.

This basic truth mandates a law-of-the-jungle approach: in order to maximize your chances of getting paid, you must make it in the self-interest of those who owe you money to pay you. You have to make yourself more trouble than you're worth. The best way to do this (legally, that is) is through the contracts you make with your customers, and the legal toolbox contains some valuable contracting tactics.

> ⇢ **This basic truth mandates a law-of-the-jungle approach: in order to maximize your chances of getting paid, you must make it in the self-interest of those who owe you money to pay you.**

I have five favorite contract clauses that can be used for this purpose in a variety of circumstances and combinations. In counseling clients over the years, I have come to refer to these as "skunk factors." A skunk has certain qualities that make its enemies think twice before making it angry. It's more trouble than it's worth. The following skunk factors can dramatically increase the likelihood that those who owe you money will look at you in the same way.

The upshot will be that big payment issues can become smaller payment issues, and that your customers, understanding how tough litigating with you will be, will opt to pay what you'll take. That translates into less time and fewer resources spent on collecting money, and more time and resources spent on making money.

**1.** *The attorneys' fee clause.* A customer owes you $100,000. It knows it has no reason not to pay you, but it figures that if it withholds payment based on some phony excuse, you'll knock off $20,000 rather than spend $20,000 on a lawyer.

Suppose, however, that the contract between you and the customer includes the following language: "In the event Customer fails to pay Company the full amount owing when due and Company commences suit in order to collect such sums, and in the event it is determined that Customer owes any sums to Company that were not paid previous to Company's commencement of such suit, then Customer shall also be required to pay all attorneys' fees and costs incurred by Company in conjunction with such suit and all collection efforts undertaken in association therewith."

Assuming the customer is solvent and knows that it will ultimately be found to owe money to you, here are the alternatives it will face: withhold payment and incur a lawsuit in which it will be required to pay not only what it owes, but also all of your counsel fees and costs, or pay you without risking this additional liability. You might still have a negotiation on your hands, but the attorneys' fees clause gives you much more leverage and the ability to play hardball. You're more trouble than you're worth.

The attorneys' fee clause can be used for purposes aside from getting paid; it works in any situation where one party might refuse to honor an obligation in the effort to cajole a meritless concession from another party. It can be of great assistance, for example, in leveraging the compliance of a tenant with its obligations under a lease, or making a licensee think twice about violating the terms of a license agreement, or keeping an investor from backing out of a funding commitment.

**2.** *The high-rate interest clause.* Same scenario, but add the following clause in the contract: "All balances are due within thirty days, and shall bear interest from that date forward at the rate of 1½ percent per month on all unpaid balances."

Delay ordinarily works in favor of whoever owes the money—he has the use of the money until he's forced to pay it. The law may make him pay some interest if he is ultimately determined to owe the money, but in many cases that simply makes the debt a low-interest, no-collateral loan. A high-rate interest clause turns that around; the cost of nonpayment becomes intolerable. Again, you become more trouble than you're worth.

Check with your lawyer on the laws that govern the right to charge interest in your jurisdiction, often called usury laws.

**3.** *The venue and jurisdiction clause.* Suppose your business is located in Pennsylvania, you deliver a product to a company in California, and they stiff you, claiming some defect or other breach on your part. If you have to chase them in California, it will cost you a lot of time and money—you'll have to retain counsel on the west coast, you'll have to travel there for depositions and trial, and so on. They know that, and they use that to bargain for a substantial discount. The same logic applies in any kind of agreement where the parties are geographically separated.

But suppose you can sue them in *your* backyard, and get the home court advantage? Now, in order for them to assert their defense to your claim for payment, they'll have to litigate in a courtroom two thousand miles away from their comfort zone . . . a major skunk factor.

Be careful. It's not always so simple to require an out-of-state company to litigate in your state, but when you can do it, it becomes a huge advantage.

**4.** *The confession of judgment clause.* In some states—*not* in all of them; check with counsel—you can include a contract provision known as a confession of judgment, or cognovit, clause. It can be used in almost any situation in which one party owes money to another and fails to pay. A confession of judgment clause goes something like this (with some further accompanying boilerplate and local variations): "In the event Smith defaults, Smith hereby irrevocably authorizes any attorney to appear in any court of competent jurisdiction and confess a judgment without process in favor of Jones and against Smith for such amount as may then appear due and owing and to consent to immediate execution against Smith upon such judgment without further process."

If you sue someone, and if you withstand the delay, expense, and rigmarole of litigation and ultimately obtain a verdict in your favor, you'll get what the law calls a judgment. A judgment is a term of art; it refers to a bundle of rights you can use to collect what you're owed. With a judgment you can sell your adversary's property, attach bank accounts, take equipment, force the disclosure of hidden assets, and so on.

A confession of judgment clause gives you a judgment *instantly*—skip the trial, and go right to the verdict. No need to discuss who's right and who's wrong; game over.

Confession of judgment clauses are hyper-technical devices; they require a lot of careful *i*-dotting and *t*-crossing by a competent attorney. When successfully utilized, however, they can end the payment debate before it starts.

**5.** *The arbitration clause.* Some people will bank on your reluctance to engage in the usual forms of litigation—file a lawsuit in the local courthouse, go through months of expensive "discovery" proceedings, go through months of expensive motion proceedings, endure the publicity, wait on a trial list for a year or two, and then endure the appeal process. They will leverage that into the so-called litigation discount.

An arbitration clause, of which there are many varieties (again, consult with counsel on which will work best in your situation), can require that all disputes be litigated in a private, confidential arbitration with reduced delays and (except in very unusual situations) no appeals. The downside is that you'll have to pay the arbitrator, which can get costly depending on the length of the hearing, but that cost is frequently outstripped by the fact that arbitration consumes less lawyer time. In the right case, arbitration reduces the overall price of litigation in both time and money and diminishes your adversary's ability to leverage an otherwise undeserved concession from you.

What you're really doing when you skillfully use skunk factors is structuring the conversation your slow-pay (or no-pay) customer will have with his attorney. Here's how it goes:

*Client*: I just got this letter threatening to sue me if I don't pay the $100,000 I owe on this last shipment. It'll cost them at least $50,000 to sue me. How about you write them back and tell them we'll settle for $50,000 right now—not a bad deal for them. I'll go to $60,000 if I have to.

*Lawyer*: Have you read this contract you signed?

*Client*: It's the usual fine-print mumbo jumbo. What difference does it make?

*Lawyer*: First of all, the contract says that if they run up $50,000 in legal fees, they get to collect that from you. So, I'm not sure your bargaining strategy is going to produce a lot of compromise on their side.

*Client*: Really? They can do that? Well, tell them to discount it for quick payment. If I pay them now, they get the use of the money and don't have to wait two years for it—$70,000 cash tomorrow. Not a penny more.

*Lawyer*: Don't think so. It says here that you owe them 1½ percent per month interest. They've got a nice little investment here, all at your expense—the more you delay, the more it's going to cost you.

*Client*: What? It says that? Look, they're in California, I'm in Pennsylvania. They don't want to spend the time to come out here, have their depositions taken, attend the trial, waste all that time. That's worth something.

*Lawyer*: Not to them. What you signed says that they can sue you in California. You'll be the one doing the traveling.

*Client*: This is ridiculous. Still, their time is money. They know how much time courtroom litigation takes—and then years of appeals. They'll be willing to give me a discount for that, won't they?

*Lawyer*: See this paragraph, the one that says Mandatory Arbitration?


Sometimes, it's good to be a skunk. All of these provisions (and others) can be used in tandem, and there are endless tweaks and alternatives. Assuming both parties are paying attention to the offers and counteroffers (sometimes these provisions do slip through unnoticed), whether you can successfully include your chosen skunk factors in an agreement depends on who has what leverage and who negotiates more skillfully.


CAUTION: A BANKRUPTCY CAN change the rules of these games.

Suppose you successfully use these skunk factors to cajole a company to pay you, and the company files for bankruptcy shortly thereafter—leaving lots of other creditors holding the bag. Delay the urge to celebrate your triumph—if the bankruptcy is filed before the expiration of what is known as the preference period (usually ninety days from the date you received payment but, in some circumstances, up to a year), your payment may be found to be a "preference," and you may be required to pay the money back pending further rulings by a bankruptcy court.

The logic of this highly contentious area of bankruptcy law is that creditors should be treated more or less equally, and therefore, a soon-to-be-bankrupt company ought not to be permitted to prefer one creditor over the other, even unintentionally. So, anyone who is paid within the preference period may have to return the money so that the bankruptcy court can divvy it up more equitably among *all* the creditors—your one hundred cents on the dollar can easily become ten cents on the dollar or nothing at all. This axiom of bankruptcy law can rear its head in unlikely contexts. Consider those who withdrew their money from Bernie Madoff less than ninety days before the Ponzi scheme was put into bankruptcy. Whether they grabbed their money out of necessity or prescience, many will find their celebrations to have been premature.

All of this is exceedingly complex. As a general rule, you need to remember that if a bankruptcy is filed, just because you were paid doesn't mean you'll be able to keep the money—so don't spend it before it's *really* yours.

## Getting Paid: How to Get Blood from a Stone

Some of the companies that owe you money will not be influenced by the leverage you can obtain through skunk factors. They will claim that they simply don't have the money, and that they're "judgment proof."

This usually plays out in one of two scenarios:

Sometimes the companies that owe you money *are* insolvent, and there are no viable collection alternatives. The first defense against that is a truly thorough and professional credit and asset analysis before the deal is made (which is a lot more than a report from a credit agency). But even that doesn't buy you much: a company that checks out as perfectly viable when you make the deal can be underwater when it's time to pay. As important as a credit check can be, it's not an insurance policy. Things change.

Sometimes the companies that owe you money are *not* insolvent, even though they say they are and even though they seem to be. You might do an asset search that comes up dry. Their accountant might provide a financial statement that looks hopeless. It will seem like you are at the end of the "I got cheated" road.

The legal toolbox provides tactics you can use in both circumstances.

*Before the money is owed: structuring the deal.* Earlier, we discussed the need to approach business situations with a healthy pessimism. In this context, that means starting your consideration of any transaction by *really* assessing the likelihood of nonpayment at some point in the future. For example, the past payment history and the apparent honesty of whom you're dealing with do matter, but even honest companies with good track records run out of money or are sold to other, not-so-honest companies. Factor in the size of the deal, consider your own tolerance for risk, and ask yourself this question: do I need a backup, a Plan B, just in case the outfit that owes me the money can't (or *says* it can't) pay me?

If the answer is yes, there are some legal toolbox techniques you can try at the onset, but they all require the other party's consent (and the assistance of counsel—these require the proper drafting of very technical documents). If the other party won't consent, it might be time to consider the wisdom of the old adage "Sometimes the best deals are the ones you don't make."

- *Personal guarantees.* Particularly when dealing with a closely held company, a personal guarantee from one or more of the owners can be valuable. Ultimately, the viability of a personal guarantee depends on the assets of the guarantor, but if nothing else, a personal guarantee tells you that an owner is willing to put his own skin in the game, which can be a key test of good faith. Personal guarantees can also help you circumvent bankruptcies—even if the company that owes you money goes bankrupt, you may still be able to keep the money paid by the nonbankrupt guarantor.

- *Affiliate guarantees.* Many businesses are broken into two or more commonly owned or overlapping entities, and the money is not always evenly distributed among them. For instance, in the construction industry, a standard strategy is for one related company to enter into contracts with customers and do the construction work, while a second related company owns all the construction equipment the first company uses and provides all the management and overhead the first company needs. The first company pays almost all its cash to the second company in equipment leasing and management fees—and when a customer or supplier tries to collect a debt from the first company, it's confronted with an empty shell.

  It's important to find out how the business you're dealing with is structured and to obtain guarantees from the affiliated entities that comprise the business. If the people you're dealing with provide the guarantees, you have a good indication that they are not playing games; if not . . . Note also that, like personal guarantees, affiliate guarantees can provide an alternate payment source if the company you dealt with files for bankruptcy.

- *Security interests in collateral.* A pledge of collateral can provide full protection *if* the collateral has value that will hold up over time—it gives you the right to take the collateral in the event of nonpayment, and it gives you a preferred status in a bankruptcy. A pledge of a certificate of deposit or other easily liquidated asset can be ideal. A pledge of receivables, inventory, stock, or some other asset that might vary in value is obviously riskier.

  In order to secure your interest in collateral, you must enter into a "security agreement" that grants you a "security interest" in the collateral, you must record that security interest in certain public offices by filing a document known as a Uniform Commercial Code Form 1 (UCC-1), and you must conform with a variety of other requirements depending on the nature of the collateral, the jurisdiction, and so on—hundreds of pages could be written on the technicalities involved in accomplishing all of this correctly and effectively. You'll want to make sure that others do not have a prior security interest. You'll need to determine whether you will remain protected in the event that, for instance, you record a security interest in inventory that is sold to a buyer or incorporated in other products. And so on . . .

Don't be dissuaded by these complications; a pledge of collateral can be *very* valuable. Just be mindful of them. Use your lawyer.

- *Mortgages on real estate.* The security agreement/UCC-1 procedure applies to what is known in the law as personalty— basically everything except real estate. To use real estate as collateral, you need to obtain a mortgage on it. As you might expect, the drafting and recording of a mortgage requires conformity with a cluster of intricate requirements, some of which will vary from location to location. Obviously, you will want to be certain that the real estate in question will maintain its value, and if you do not hold the first mortgage, you need to factor in the impediments to turning the real estate into cash. Talk to counsel.

- *Letters of credit and bonds.* An excellent source of security is a letter of credit or a bond—basically, these are like taking out an insurance policy on your debt. If whoever owes you the money does not pay you, the party who issued the letter of credit or bond (normally a bank, insurance company, or similar institution) is then required to step up to the plate and write a check. These documents are among the most esoteric and impenetrable of legal instruments—but if handled by competent counsel, they can work wonders.

The practical problem with these devices, however, is that you usually can't get them if you need them. Before a financial institution will issue a letter of credit or a bond insuring payment from $A$ to $B$, it will want to assure itself that $A$ will have the assets with which to reimburse the financial institution for payments made to $B$. If, for instance, you are insisting that your customer secure its debt to you with a letter of credit or bond because your customer has limited assets, your customer probably won't be able to acquire either one.

Still, letters of credit and bonds can be of great value (and can be lifesavers in a bankruptcy). If, for instance, your customer is cash poor but real estate rich, it might be able to get a letter of credit or bond (albeit for a hefty price). If your customer fails to pay you, you can draw on the letter of credit or bond and leave it to the financial institution that issued the instrument to obtain reimbursement by converting your customer's real estate assets into cash—often a lengthy and expensive process.

WHEN THE DEAL GOES BAD: *chasing the money.* Let's suppose you're now past the planning stage—you made a deal, and you haven't been paid. The other side tells you that as much as it would like to pay you, it can't—the well is dry. Do you have meaningful options?

The legal toolbox does contain some underused ploys and maneuvers. But there are no guarantees they'll get you anywhere. Whether you spend the time and money required to explore these possibilities (and some will be a lot less taxing than others) depends on whether there is some reason to believe you'll eventually find a pocket with some money in it, the amount in question, and your appetite for throwing good money after bad, since that's how things may turn out.

Some businesses I've represented want no part of collection efforts. If a few rounds of letters and telephone calls don't work, they'll chalk their loss up to experience and walk away. Perhaps they will refer it to a collection firm with the proviso that no litigation be instituted. Others, usually acting out of anger or embarrassment, will tell me to do anything and everything the law allows, whether or not it makes no financial sense. Most will work with me to see if we can turn up any tangible indications that the investment of time and money in the collection effort will be worth the payoff, they'll factor in the amount in question, and they'll set a reasonable budget and turn me loose.

···➔ **Whether you spend the time and money required to explore these possibilities (and some will be a lot less taxing than others) depends on whether there is some reason to believe you'll eventually find a pocket with some money in it, the amount in question, and your appetite for throwing good money after bad, since that's how things may turn out.**

Here are some options the law provides. Discuss them with counsel based on the particular circumstances you face:

*Insist on a judgment.* As we talked about previously, a judgment is what you get when you file a lawsuit and win. Once you have a judgment against a company, you have an arsenal of powerful weapons at your disposal that you can use to search for assets and take them once you find them.

If the people you're dealing with claim that their company has no assets, ask that they voluntarily consent to the entry of a judgment against the company. After all, you'll say, if the company really has no assets, what difference would it make? If the company really is "judgment proof," why resist the entry of a judgment?

If they do it, they're telling you that so far as they know the company really is insolvent. But if they don't, you've got some reason to be suspicious and a rational basis to get more aggressive.

*Get the tax returns and loan applications.* Those in charge of a company that owes you money might be willing to lie to you, but they're usually less willing to lie to the IRS. Ask for copies of the company's most recent tax returns, subject to a confidentiality agreement. If the company claims that it doesn't want to provide the returns because they include personal or private information, tell it you're willing to go along with reasonable redactions.

Also, ask for copies of the company's most recent loan applications and financial statements provided to banks or other lenders. When a company applies for a loan, it will generally try to portray itself in the best possible light and for that reason will reveal the assets it might otherwise try to hide. This is where you may find the assets that would not be so obvious in other documents, such as off-the-books loans payable by the company's officers, beach homes owned by the company for "business entertainment" but used by the officers, license agreements or pending patents the company believes to be of particular value, and so on.

If the people you're dealing with won't make these disclosures while, at the same time, claiming that their company has no assets, you have some reason to believe you're being misled.

*File suit and see if they defend.* It doesn't cost that much to file a lawsuit. You can always withdraw it later. If you sue a company that claims to have no assets, and the company hires counsel and aggressively defends, the people who run it are telling you that they have something to lose.

*Consider "successor liability."* In 2000, Wanda Cash and Mark Down, wealthy entrepreneurs, formed CashDown Inc. for the purpose of making small business loans. They each invested $250,000 in the company, and thanks to the contacts they had made over the years, they located willing and solvent borrowers and earned a substantial return.

Seeking to expand in 2002, Cash and Down sought and obtained a $10 million line of credit from Last National Bank in order to increase their lending capacity. From 2002 through 2008, they were wildly successful, but in 2009, CashDown Inc. was caught in the recession—it had taken down $5 million on its line, loaned it out, and could only collect $2 million. Last National quickly confessed judgment against CashDown Inc. for the $3 million debt. At that point, Cash and Down concluded that there was no point in continuing to operate the company—even if they could obtain more money to loan, every dime they made would be attached by Last National before it reached them. In effect, they'd be working for Last National, not themselves.

- *Scenario One:* A month later, Down and Cash convince a private equity firm, Kresch & Byrne, that they learned valuable lessons from CashDown Inc.'s mistakes and had developed new contacts and lending criteria that would ensure future success. Kresch & Byrne do some due diligence, they like what they see, and they tell Cash and Down that they will make a $5 million line of credit available to them. Cash and Down form a new company— WanMar Loans Inc., which successfully picks up where CashDown left off and makes a ton of money.

- *Scenario Two:* Cash and Down are unable to secure a new lender, so they make a deal with an investor, Hugh Meaney. Meaney agrees to provide a $5 million line of credit in exchange for 35 percent of the profits and veto power over all lending decisions. Cash and Down form WanMar Loans Inc., sign the appropriate contracts with Meaney, and WanMar Loans makes a ton of money.

- *Scenario Three:* Cash and Down are unable to secure a new funding source, so they sell CashDown Inc.'s assets (its name, goodwill, office and equipment leases, customer files . . .) to CashDown LLC, a company formed by Hugh Meaney for the purpose of doing what CashDown Inc. used to do. Meaney doesn't know anything about operating the business—he's simply looking for a return on his money—so he hires Cash and Down to run the company in exchange for a 10 percent ownership interest, a generous salary, and a hefty bonus program. Meaney makes a $5 million line of credit available, Cash and Down do their jobs well, and everyone makes a ton of money.

Last National's CEO, Len D'Amore, was understandably angry about the bad loan to CashDown Inc. He ultimately became aware of Wanda Cash's and Mark Down's success, and asked the bank's controller to investigate the bank's options. The controller confirmed that the loan was made only to CashDown Inc., that CashDown Inc. had, in fact, gone out of business, and that Last National had stupidly failed to obtain personal guarantees or other security for the debt. D'Amore was frustrated and disappointed, but set aside his emotions so he could look at things objectively, from a dollars-and-cents perspective. Not wishing to throw good money after bad chasing a defunct company, he fired the Last National lending officer responsible for the CashDown Inc. loan, notified Last National's board about the loss, and closed the file.

Did D'Amore make the right call?

Sometimes businesses fail despite the best efforts of the people who own and operate them. As a matter of public policy, however, we recognize that the consequences of a business failure must be confined to the business that failed; otherwise, if every business failure meant personal ruin, few would ever take the risks inherent in business ownership, and that would devastate our economy. The law gives business owners the opportunity to conduct their businesses through certain kinds of limited liability entities, like corporations, limited liability companies, and limited liability partnerships. In the law's eyes, these entities are like separate persons, each with their own assets and liabilities. So long as the proper *i*'s are dotted and *t*'s are crossed, a business that operates through one of these entities can only lose what it owns—the separate assets of those who own the entity are protected (unless, for instance, they signed a personal guarantee or pledged their own collateral). If the business fails, the owners can live to fight another day.

But there's another side to that coin: as is so often the case, the laws that are meant to protect honest people can be abused by dishonest people.

Picture a situation in which John Jones owes money to a bank. He changes his name to Sam Smith and claims he is now off the hook—after all, he says, John Jones is the one who owes the money, and I'm Sam Smith. The law, of course, would not allow Jones to escape his obligations through a mere change of identity; no matter what he calls himself, he's still the one who owes the money.

The same sort of thing happens when it comes to business entities. Like John Jones, a company cannot escape its liabilities merely by changing its name. But beyond that, what about a situation where a company goes out of business before it can pay all of its debts, and the owners then form and operate a new company that does the same thing with the same assets and the same people in the same place in the same way? The creditors get stiffed, even though the business, albeit through another entity, is making money.

That, the law generally says, is the functional equivalent of a name change—under a legal doctrine known as "successor liability," the new company will be held responsible for the debts of the old company. Otherwise, each time a company ran up a debt, the owners could simply start a new company and do it all over again. Without the successor liability doctrine, business would become a legalized shell game.

Now consider a situation in which a company sells its assets to another company that is owned by a previously uninvolved third party. The new company conducts the same kind of business as the old company, but there's new ownership, new management, and a new location. That's a typical, arm's-length business asset sale, and the new company will not be liable for the old company's debts—the doctrine of successor liability should not and does not reach that far. Otherwise, it would be very difficult to sell a business—the new owners would always be burdened by the sins of the old owners.

The real difficulties lie in between those ends of the transactional continuum.

Consider *Scenario One*. WanMar Loans has a new funding source and some new and better business procedures, but in most courtrooms in most jurisdictions, the doctrine of successor liability will hold it responsible for CashDown Inc.'s debts. Cash and Down messed up by thinking otherwise, and Len D'Amore, the CEO of Last National, messed up by walking away.

Consider *Scenario Two*. Now there's someone else involved in the business—CashDown Inc. and WanMar Loans Inc. are no longer exactly the same . . . but they're close. Maybe WanMar Loans will be held liable for CashDown's debts, maybe not; different states have their own, nuanced definitions of the successor liability doctrine. Sometimes it boils down to a judge's or jury's view on whether the third party, Hugh Meaney in this case, was an honest entrepreneur looking for an honest deal or whether he was a willing participant in a scheme to cheat creditors of the old company. Cash, Down, and Meaney messed up by not structuring their deal in a way that would build a higher wall between CashDown Inc. and WanMar Loans Inc., and D'Amore messed up by not having counsel take a harder look at the possibilities.

···▹ **The creativity of our greatest writers often pales by comparison to the creativity of our greatest scam artists. This fact has led to a parade of dishonest, though ingenious and innovative, corporate structures, followed by a series of equally ingenious and innovative adjustments in the law's responses, often through mutations in the successor liability doctrine.**

Consider *Scenario Three*. Now Cash and Down are minority participants, and a new company that is majority-owned and controlled by a new player is in charge. CashDown LLC should be safe, and D'Amore probably made the right call.

The creativity of our greatest writers often pales by comparison to the creativity of our greatest scam artists. This fact has led to a parade of dishonest, though ingenious and innovative, corporate structures, followed by a series of equally ingenious and innovative adjustments in the law's responses, often through mutations in the successor liability doctrine. The resultant body of law is extensive, and growing all the time. However, all you really need to remember is this: If you discover (and finding out is often the hardest part) that the people who ran the company that owes you money are now involved in a new and similar enterprise, consider that a red flag, and consult counsel. Things might not be as hopeless as they seem.

*Look for "fraudulent conveyances."* Suppose Wanda Cash and Mark Down had signed personal guarantees and were now personally on the hook for the $3 million owed to Last National Bank. Cash and Down hire a consulting firm, Hyde & Sikh, which advertises itself as "expert asset protection counselors," to provide advice. Hyde & Sikh prepares and implements a detailed plan involving the transfer of Cash's and Down's money and valuables into a web of spurious trusts and phony offshore companies, all to make it appear that they have limited assets.

Last National's CEO, Len D'Amore, meets with Cash and Down to discuss how they wish to handle their obligations under their personal guarantees. Cash and Down each bring audited financial statements (prepared by Hyde & Sikh's affiliated accounting firm). The financial statements, inclusive of Hyde & Sikh's "asset protection" strategies, show that Cash and Down each have a net worth of less than $100,000. Things have been tough, they explain. The recession has taken a toll.

Many creditors in D'Amore's position would review the financials, throw up their hands, and take what they could get. After all, the financial statements were *audited*. They *must* be accurate.

Smarter creditors in D'Amore's position, aside from recognizing the realistic limits of an audit, would think twice. When dealing with the formerly rich who are now the apparently not-so-rich, the proper initial response is skepticism, not acceptance. The issue is not limited to what their financial status is at the time they report it, though the veracity of their disclosures always bears investigating; the issue is *also* how it got that way, which implicates the search for what the law calls fraudulent conveyances.

The law of fraudulent conveyances is (surprise, surprise) complex, but the underlying concept is a simple one. You owe the bank $500,000. You have a $100,000 certificate of deposit, $200,000 in cash, and a cabin in the mountains that's worth $200,000—all of which you'd like to hang on to. So, you transfer the certificate of deposit and the $200,000 to a trust you set up for your children, and you transfer the cabin to your spouse, all in compliance with the purported advice of your estate planning attorney. Presto—you have no assets left, and the bank's out of luck.

As you might expect, it's not that easy. A court would likely find these transfers to be "fraudulent conveyances." The hallmark of a fraudulent conveyance is, basically, a transfer made when you owe money to creditors, for which you receive less than fair value in return, leaving you without the assets to pay what you owe. The significance? If a creditor is successful in having a court label the transfer a fraudulent conveyance, the creditor can turn back time and reverse the transfer—the assets you transferred must be returned to you (which can cause significant hardship for whomever you transferred to), and the creditor can take those assets in satisfaction of your debt.

It all sounds simple and routine in this kind of obvious context, but in the world of business transactions, it can become complicated and convoluted.

Here's an archetypal example: A company owes you a substantial debt but claims it cannot pay because it is on the brink of insolvency. Your lawyer subpoenas the company's general ledger and hires a forensic accountant to search for suspicious entries. The accountant finds repeated payments from the company to a management consulting firm. On a hunch, your lawyer subpoenas the records of the management consulting firm and starts taking depositions— and ultimately confirms that the company owns the management consulting firm. Under the guise of paying for management consulting services, which it never received, the company was essentially transferring money to itself, a classic fraudulent conveyance.

This kind of scheme finds its way into a variety of contexts—overpayments to phony suppliers, independent contractors, whatever. Those payments can be reversed, and if the money can't be found, the door might be open to a panoply of other remedies available for the fraudulent abuse of limited liability entities generally, detailed below.

Here's another common scheme: The company that owes you money owns its own building. However, it has almost no equity in the property—the public records reflect that it gave a sizable mortgage on the building to a financial institution with an unfamiliar name. Your lawyer probes and confirms that the financial institution is owned by a corporation that ultimately traces back to the company you're trying to collect from and that the mortgage is a sham. A mortgage is a transfer of an asset—an interest in real property—and it can be voided under fraudulent conveyance laws.

And so on, and so on . . . again, greed motivates stupendous creativity. Before accepting a financial bath from a debtor who has made a convenient transition from rich to not-so-rich, look for the fraudulent conveyances. The legal toolbox provides creditors who hold judgments with some potent investigative weapons that can be used to determine the assets in a debtor's possession at a particular point in time, and the ultimate disposition of each of those assets thereafter. If there's enough in question to justify the investigative investment, the search for fraudulent conveyances can reveal hidden treasure.

> **Before accepting a financial bath from a debtor who has made a convenient transition from rich to not-so-rich, look for the fraudulent conveyances.**

One more point: In many jurisdictions, those who "aid and abet" in the creation and implementation of fraudulent conveyances and similar schemes can be held liable to the creditors who are cheated in the process. It's another option worth considering.

*Consider "piercing the corporate veil."* As discussed previously, as a matter of public policy, those who own a limited liability entity (corporate shareholders, LLC members, LLP partners . . .) are not personally liable for the entity's debts and obligations. The same is true for those who are responsible for operating the entity—officers, directors, and so on. The limited liability entity and the individuals who own and operate it are effectively viewed as different persons. As the law has phrased it for centuries, those individuals stand behind "the corporate veil."

But there is an exception that, as usual, was developed as a counterpoint to the incessant schemes of those who have tried to corrupt the law's well-intended protections. In certain circumstances, you can pierce the corporate veil and hold the owners and/or operators of a limited liability entity responsible for the debts and liabilities of the entity. Piercing the corporate veil can be a fabulously effective tactic: nothing seems to turn up previously undiscoverable corporate assets faster than a credible threat to collect a liability out of the personal pockets of the corporation's shareholders or directors.

···❯ **Piercing the corporate veil can be a fabulously effective tactic: nothing seems to turn up previously undiscoverable corporate assets faster than a credible threat to collect a liability out of the personal pockets of the corporation's shareholders or directors.**

The right to pierce the corporate veil and attack those who stand behind an entity generally arises in two contexts: First, some entity owners (typically, small businesses) treat their company's money and assets as if they were their own—personal and business funds are consistently commingled, the company regularly pays for the owners' personal expenses, loans to the owners are unaccounted for, and so on. Essentially, the law says that if the owners and operators of a company don't treat it like a separate entity, neither will the law.

Second, the law will react to company owners and operators who use a limited liability entity for fraudulent, deceptive, or otherwise dishonest purposes. The law created the concept of a limited liability entity for all the right reasons and will not allow its protective shield to be used for all the wrong reasons.

Again, the boundless resourcefulness of those trying to escape their debts has produced an astonishing variety of corporate contrivances and machinations. Successor schemes such as those discussed previously are commonplace—do business in entity *A*, run up a debt, shut the doors, and move on to entity *B*. In many of these cases, the creditors will not only be able to hold both entities liable for the debt, they'll also be able to pierce the corporate veil and hold the owners and operators who perpetrated the scheme liable as well. The same is true with respect to the fraudulent conveyance tactics discussed in the preceding section: incur a liability, clean out the available assets through bogus transfers, and claim insolvency. Using limited liability entities to front Ponzi schemes will result in piercing the corporate veil cases. So, too, will instances in which business owners and operators knowingly sell defective or counterfeit goods and hide behind a limited liability entity to defraud their customers.

The point is this: If you're stuck with a liability owed by a worthless entity, you might be out of luck. But you might not be, so don't be so quick to walk away. If the dollars make sense, have counsel take a closer look. Collecting money is all about leverage, and if you can pull back the veil and expose the people behind the company to a realistic risk, your leverage increases dramatically.

*Do you have a fraud claim—and can you go after the people who misled you?* Let's suppose you're dealing with the executive vice president of sales in a reputable and well-run company. The EVP tells you that the $200,000 piece of equipment he's trying to sell you is perfect for your application. In fact, he knows it's not—he knows it will not do what you need it to do, that it has major problems, and that a new and better model will be out in six months. He needs the commission now, though, so he lies. You believe him, the equipment fails, and you suffer significant losses.

Setting aside the "my word against your word" issue (will you be able to prove what he told you?), in *some* jurisdictions, when purposeful misrepresentations of this type are made, you can go after the company for fraud. Sparing you the technicalities, a fraud claim creates a risk of punitive damages, which can increase your leverage. This is not permitted in all states—some states say that except in truly extreme circumstances, if the deal arises out of a contract, you can only bring a breach of contract lawsuit in which punitive damages are not allowed. Consult with counsel.

Even better, in *some* jurisdictions, you can also go after the EVP *himself* for fraud. That, too, creates leverage: if you can create a palpable risk to the EVP's personal assets, he'll do all he can to get the company to resolve the case and get him off the hook. The potential for this sort of claim often becomes apparent when a seller tries to collect from a buyer. Suppose you're selling a piece of equipment to a company. It agrees to pay 50 percent in advance but asks for the right to pay the balance sixty days after delivery. You ask for some assurances about the company's solvency. The president of the company tells you that it just obtained a major contract and will be flush with cash by the time payment is due. It turns out to be a lie, and you get stiffed. Think about a fraud claim against the company *and* the individual who purposefully misled you.

Note: some states have special statutes that provide amplified remedies in situations involving fraud or other dishonest practices. These statutes sometimes allow for double and triple damages, injunctions, attorneys' fees, and other remedies.

*Put a company into an involuntary bankruptcy.* It's usually bad news when a company that owes you money goes into bankruptcy. But not always.

Earlier, we discussed bankruptcy "preference periods" and how they can work against you. For instance, if you successfully cajole a payment out of a company, you might have to return it if they file for bankruptcy within ninety days after you get paid. This concept, however, can work for you. Suppose a company owes you money, you aren't being paid, but you hear it is paying other, more favored creditors . . . and that it might then go out of business. Now this whole "preference period" business makes sense: shouldn't the company's remaining assets be shared equally among the creditors, instead of being doled out to a favored few?

Bankruptcy law and procedure is a very, *very* specialized area of the law, replete with layers of exceptions, conditions, and complexities. It's a classic "don't try this at home" endeavor. Here's all you need to know on this point for now: in some situations, you can force a company into an "involuntary bankruptcy" and thereby trigger the "preference period" protections, assuming you do it in time. It's an option you need to be aware of; talk to counsel.

## Avoiding Disputes: Define the Deal; Specify the Specifications

Companies sell goods and/or services and buy goods and/or services. Disputes about whether you provided what you were supposed to provide, and whether you got what you were supposed to get, are huge time and money wasters.

⇢ **Disputes about whether you provided what you were supposed to provide, and whether you got what you were supposed to get, are huge time and money wasters.**

The issue arises in different ways: In some instances, the parties never communicate about all of the important parts to the transaction—too much is left unsaid. In other instances, the parties do communicate, but don't get it in writing and have (or purport to have) contrary versions of what was said (the "my word against your word" problem). In still other instances, the parties do get it in writing, but the writing is vague, incomplete, or susceptible to different interpretations.

These disputes typically do not involve the fundamentals; the parties normally nail those down. In an agreement to buy and sell steel trim pieces or air filters or hard hats, there usually isn't a dispute over price or quantity. In an agreement to buy and sell management consulting, process improvement, or training services, there usually isn't a dispute over the amount of the fee and who will provide the services.

And then there's the rest of it . . .

"But, you said the steel trim pieces were heat resistant, and they're not. No way we're paying for these."

"We needed air filters with a higher airflow rate—we put these into our equipment, and now our customers are complaining left and right. We're holding you responsible."

"You told me that these hard hats would provide protection for ten thousand volts. We've got a real problem."

"Wasn't the management consulting supposed to deal with our general ledger *and* our inventory-tracking system? I'm not paying the final 50 percent until that part is completed to our satisfaction."

"Our costs only dropped 2 percent since the process-improvement work—you promised us substantial cost savings. We're holding you responsible for the $300,000 in savings we expected."

"The training was fine, but we just got sued for sexual harassment—and the guy who did it was one of the guys you trained. We think you're responsible."

The key to avoiding these kinds of disputes is to take the time and use (or obtain) the expertise required to foresee the not-so-obvious-but-still-foreseeable problems. Go beyond the price/quantity terms, utilize some healthy pessimism, ask yourself the basic questions, and take the time to *really* think about the answers. Might they be expecting something more or different than what we are providing? What might go wrong? Am I certain I've protected myself and that I can prove it?

> ⋯⇥ Go beyond the price/quantity terms, utilize some healthy pessimism, ask yourself the basic questions, and take the time to *really* think about the answers. Might they be expecting something more or different than what we are providing? What might go wrong? Am I certain I've protected myself and that I can prove it?

Once you've thought the situation through, you need to put a contract in place that covers you. Sometimes standard product specifications or a boilerplate "what's provided/what's not" consulting services description can do the job. Sometimes, particularly when detailed negotiations ensue, a custom-drafted document will be necessary. Sometimes e-mail can be used to fill in the holes.

You'll need to foreclose the "I know that's what the paperwork says, but you told me that . . ." problem that foments so many commercial disputes. You'll usually need counsel to help you through the contracting process and to lock in the language that will stand up to a future challenge.

When the other side claims the deal required heat resistance or high-voltage protection or inventory-control analysis, your goal is to put yourself in a position in which you can show them that, in fact, the deal required no such thing. Ultimately, you want to stack the deck so that when your customer consults with its counsel, irate and indignant, it will be told that it doesn't have a case. The result: a mountain becomes a molehill; a battle is avoided.

## Minimize Your Exposure: Warranty and Damage Disclaimers

Stuff happens. You might make a mistake. You might be unable to provide what you promised. You might, in short, screw up. Or, almost as bad, the other side might be able to prove you screwed up even if you didn't. The legal toolbox has some reliable approaches that can minimize your exposure. The task here is twofold: first, you need to redefine what constitutes a screwup; second, you need to lower the price of a screwup.

> ⇢ Stuff happens. You might make a mistake. You might be unable to provide what you promised. You might, in short, screw up. Or, almost as bad, the other side might be able to prove you screwed up even if you didn't. The legal toolbox has some reliable approaches that can minimize your exposure.

The first task involves an adjunct to what was discussed in the preceding section: when the other side complains because your product failed after three years or only processes five units a minute or because your service did not result in sales increases or morale improvements, you want to have the right, if you choose, to walk away. To do this, your contract has to include a provision that effectively says that your written statements about your product or service—what the law calls your warranties—are all there is, and you're not responsible for anything beyond that. The equipment failed after three years? Sorry, but I'm not liable for that. Your sales did not increase as a result of my consulting services? Sorry, but that's not my problem.

The contract provision that can give you this option is a "warranty disclaimer." Effectively, it says that you "disclaim" (that is, eliminate your responsibility for) all other warranties about your product or service beyond those you've agreed to set forth in writing. You've probably seen these provisions in the sales documents for everything from your tires to your personal computer. Among a litany of other boilerplate, there's usually a phrase something like, "There are no other warranties, express or implied, other than as set forth in writing herein." In certain contexts, a warranty disclaimer must be in bold type, and must include specific language disclaiming certain "implied warranties"—all of which involve legal explanations beyond the scope of this book. Particularly in the case of consumer products, there are limitations on what can be disclaimed.

The second task involves damage control. Here's the nightmare (but all too common) scenario in conceptual terms: You sell industrial gears. A factory comes to you and tells you that it needs a set of gears for its production line—and it better be right, because if there's a problem, the line cannot operate. You provide the gears, they turn out to be defective, and they fail. Your customer's production line is shut down until you can replace the gears, which takes a week. The gears cost $10,000. Your customer loses $1,000,000 in profits as the result of the shutdown and sues you for its losses.

These kinds of damages are called consequential damages—they result as the consequence of some breach or other failure. You can disclaim responsibility for most of these (and many other) kinds of damages. Again, you've probably seen the language, something like, "Buyer's remedies shall be limited to the cost of repair or replacement, at Seller's sole option. Under no circumstances shall Seller be liable for any incidental, consequential, or other damages of any kind, including without limitation lost profits."

If properly done, depending on the context, and so long as you can get the other side to agree, a damage disclaimer can relieve you of responsibility if a defective product or service causes a serious injury, results in a fire, puts a company out of business, and so on. Again, mountains become molehills, and serious battles become manageable arguments. There are exceptions. This is technical stuff that requires counsel in order to make certain the disclaimer is enforceable when the time comes. But the important point is to know these options are out there. Warning: Be careful if the shoe is on the other foot. When you buy goods or services, the warranty and damage disclaimers that your seller tries to include in the deal can cripple you. The question is whose mountain turns into a molehill, and who gets to choose which battles are fought on whose terms?

⇢ **Warning: Be careful if the shoe is on the other foot. When you buy goods or services, the warranty and damage disclaimers that your seller tries to include in the deal can cripple you. The question is whose mountain turns into a molehill, and who gets to choose which battles are fought on whose terms?**

## Manage Your Exposure: Contractual Stopgaps

Disclaimers can eliminate or limit claims that an adverse party can make against you. If you can't work a warranty and/or damage disclaimer into the deal, however, you should consider some other techniques that can help you manage, if not avoid altogether, your potential exposure.

*Notice and opportunity to cure.* If you're the one providing a product or service, you'll want to try to work in a provision that requires the other side to notify you of a potential breach and give you an opportunity to fix it before things spin into litigation. For instance, if you sell a piece of equipment, and the buyer claims it doesn't perform as specified, you would want the buyer to state the problem and give you a chance to make it right. If you provided programming services and your customer claims there's a glitch, you would want the opportunity to fix it before the customer hires another consultant and tries to stick you with the bill.

*Grace period.* Anytime you're subject to a deadline, try to insert a "grace period" into the deal. If you committed to make a payment or a delivery by a specific date, try to obtain a cushion to protect against bureaucratic delays or mistakes. If the other side won't go along with it, try to cap your liability—*X* dollars per day for each day of delay. Lawyers who deal in this area can bring a variety of creative approaches to the bargaining table.

*Alternative dispute resolution.* Alternative dispute resolution (ADR) allows parties to custom design how their potential disagreement will be handled.

For instance, sometimes a party to a contract will start a lawsuit out of anger, not reason. To protect against this, many companies will insist on a contract provision that requires any party with a gripe to submit it to a mandatory mediation procedure before filing suit—both sides will then be required to meet with a neutral third party in the effort to resolve their differences. This kind of mandated cool-down period can be invaluable in taking the heat out of a dispute and allowing the parties to focus on a solution instead of immediately starting a war.

In the case of disagreements that can't be settled, some companies prefer arbitration over a public jury trial for the reasons discussed previously—for instance, in the right case, arbitrations can be quicker and cheaper with less chance of adverse publicity. Sometimes, companies will be willing to go to court, but they want to avoid a trial by jury and will insist that all trials be heard by a judge without a jury (for instance, in a dispute brought by an employee against an employer where jury sympathy might tilt toward the "little guy").

All of these options, and many more, can be inserted into the offer-counteroffer-acceptance contract negotiation process (though, in some cases, particularly those involving consumers and certain federal employment rights, there can be limitations). Alternative dispute resolution is burgeoning in popularity. Experienced attorneys will be able to advise you on the options to traditional litigation and how to draft an ADR provision that will withstand judicial scrutiny.

*Contractual statute of limitations.* A "statute of limitations" is the legal term for the deadline by which different kinds of lawsuits must be commenced; if you don't file your lawsuit by the expiration of the statute of limitations, you lose your rights. The deadline varies depending on the type of claim and from state to state. Typically, the statute of limitations for breach of contract claims will be something on the order of four to six years from the date of the breach, and the statute of limitations for fraud and negligence claims will be in the range of two to four years from the date of the wrongful conduct. Many jurisdictions also utilize a "discovery rule," which provides that the statute of limitations does not begin to run until the aggrieved party is on notice of the facts that comprise the claim.

Imagine a situation in which a company provides a manufacturing system to a customer and there are arguments about whether the system functions as promised. In a jurisdiction where the statute of limitations on breach of contract cases is six years, that's how long the company that provided the system will have to wait before knowing for certain if it's going to get sued. In a jurisdiction where the discovery rule applies, the potential for litigation could hang over the company's head for many years longer.

A potential solution is a contractual statute of limitations—that is, an agreement between the parties that no matter what the law says, all claims must be brought within six months of the date the installation is completed. If you're the provider of a product or service, the upside of a contractual statute of limitations is, obviously, that it limits the timeframe within which you have to worry; the downside is that it may provoke your customer to file a lawsuit even though it ultimately might not have done so had it had a longer time to let things play themselves out. Talk to counsel.

## Liquidated Damages

If you enter into a contract with someone, and he breaches that contract, you can recover the damages the breach caused you to suffer. But the law says that you can only recover the amount of damages you can actually prove. You're not allowed to speculate; it's all about *proof*, and if you can't prove it, you can't recover it.

There are many business situations where a breached deal creates a measurable amount of damages. You agree to purchase one thousand gizmos at $8 each. Your supplier backs out. You end up buying them from another supplier at $10 each—your damages are $2 per gizmo, or $2,000. Moore Company agrees to deliver by a specific date, and because it doesn't, Goode Manufacturing loses a multimillion-dollar deal.

But there are other situations where a breached agreement will hurt you, perhaps a great deal, but you can't prove the amount of damages the breach caused you to suffer. For example, let's say you're a consultant, and you get into a dispute with a client. You think the client's wrong, but you're willing to pay some money to avoid the legal fees and wasted time. However, you demand that the settlement be kept confidential—if it gets out, it could make you look like you did something wrong and hurt your reputation. You enter into a confidentiality agreement in which your client pledges not to disclose the existence or terms of the settlement to anyone outside of your client's company.

A few months later, you're pitching a new client, and in the course of the conversation, you learn that he heard about the settlement. You ask how he obtained his information, and it turns out that in violation of the confidentiality agreement, the president of your former client let it slip.

You're livid. And to make things worse, the job you were pitching ends up going to one of your competitors. But you can't prove why you didn't get the job; maybe they just liked your competitor more than you. You don't want to involve the client you were pitching in the dispute by, for example, taking the depositions of their decision makers in the lawsuit you commence against your former client—*that* will ensure that you never get another shot at business. You're in a situation where you've suffered a wrong, but you can't quantify your loss.

Or suppose you enter into a non-solicitation agreement with your CFO, providing that if the CFO leaves your company, he will not solicit any of your employees to go with him. He quits, forms his own company, and violates the agreement—he solicits his former assistant, who immediately joins him. You speak to the former assistant, and he says that even if he were never solicited, he would have contacted his old boss and left you to join him at the first opportunity.

So the fact that your former CFO solicited his assistant really didn't cause you any damages; you would have lost that employee no matter what . . . or, at least, that's their story. Your former CFO thumbed his nose at his commitment, and you've got no claim.

How do you protect yourself against these kinds of situations? You could foresee how this sort of thing would happen when you entered into the confidentiality agreement and non-solicitation agreement. Is there anything you could have done to get yourself some compensation and, at the same time, create a deterrent that might keep the other side in line?

The legal toolbox has an answer—the liquidated damages clause.

A liquidated damages clause is a contract provision that requires the breaching party to pay the non-breaching party a defined sum of money—it does not depend on proof of actual damages. "Smith shall pay Jones $5,000 for each instance in which Smith breaches any of the obligations set forth in this Agreement." If the other side violates the commitment, you get paid, even though you can't prove the amount of money you lost as the result of the breach.

> ⇢ **A liquidated damages clause is a contract provision that requires the breaching party to pay the non-breaching party a defined sum of money—it does not depend on proof of actual damages.**

Courts will enforce a liquidated damages provision only if there is a reasonable connection between the actual damages suffered and the amount of the liquidated damages the breaching party is required to pay. In a contract, you cannot impose what amounts to a penalty or fine; contracts are not enforceable if their purpose is to punish as opposed to compensate. But so long as a court concludes that the intent of the parties was to come up with something that would fairly compensate the non-breaching party, given the difficulties of proving actual damages, it will enforce the clause. It's generally a matter of degree.

You should work with a lawyer to maximize the likelihood that the liquidated damages provision will withstand scrutiny—there are some drafting techniques that will increase the odds. But the point is that if you are in a situation where you can foresee that damages will be tough to prove if the other side fails to do what it's supposed to do, a properly drafted liquidated damages option can be a tidy and profitable remedy.

## The Battle of the Forms

Recall the mirror image rule, which requires that in order to form a contract, the offer and acceptance must be the mirror images of each other; otherwise, the acceptance is a rejection and, perhaps, a counteroffer, and the negotiation process proceeds until there's an exact match.

But that's not always how it works in the real world.

Let's suppose you're running P2P Enterprises. You're committed to minimizing as many customer-related disputes and risks as you can, preferring to spend time finding new customers, not fighting with old customers. You meet with P2P Enterprises's lawyer, you muster a healthy pessimism, and you begin the planning process.

You decide the best way to proceed is to develop a standard form, the P2P Terms and Conditions. You will include it in every deal with every customer, and it will make everything clear right up front. You make sure that at the top of the form it says in large, bold type, "All purchases of P2P's products are governed by the P2P Terms and Conditions." Just to be sure, the form also says that by placing an order and accepting delivery, every customer agrees to be bound by the P2P Terms and Conditions.

In terms of content, you want to get as much leverage as you can in the event of a slow-paying customer, so you include provisions requiring the customer to pay you interest on overdue accounts. You don't want to chase customers all over the country, and you don't want to deal with judges and juries, so you include a provision requiring all disputes to be arbitrated in your home city. You're concerned that customers will expect too much from the P2P, and you don't want to be stuck with what some overeager salesperson might have said to a customer, so you include detailed specifications describing what the P2P will and will not do, and you state that these specifications supersede all statements made by any P2P Enterprises employee. You also include a warranty disclaimer clearly stating that you are making no other warranties of any kind and a damage disclaimer providing that you are not responsible for consequential damages, such as lost profits or increased expenses.

You breathe a sigh of relief. Thank goodness for the legal toolbox, you think.

Except for one thing—your customers have lawyers and they, too, know all about the legal toolbox.

The following week, your sales department receives a letter from a major university on the opposite coast—it's committed to environmental responsibility, and it wants to know how much you'll charge them for one hundred P2Ps. The last paragraph of the letter says the following: "This offer to purchase shall be subject to the University Terms and Conditions attached hereto." Accompanying the letter is a page of fine-print, legal-sounding doubletalk. No one in the sales department pays any attention—they see stuff like that all the time and know it doesn't mean anything. In response, following the new procedures you and your lawyer have established, your sales department sends a quotation along with a cover letter that says, "This offer to sell is governed by the P2P Terms and Conditions enclosed herewith."

The university receives the quotation, likes the price, and sends its purchase order, including the following in bold type at the top: "This purchase order is an offer to purchase and is subject to the University Terms and Conditions attached hereto, and shall be immediately returned if the Seller does not agree to same in full."

Your salespeople are excited, and send the standard form confirmation prepared by your lawyer which, at the top, says the following in equally bold type: "Your purchase order is acknowledged and this confirmation constitutes an offer to sell subject to the P2P Terms and Conditions enclosed herewith."

The P2Ps are ultimately delivered. The deal was 50 percent down, the balance sixty days after delivery. One month after delivery, the university sends you a letter complaining that the P2Ps only provided $20,000 and not the $40,000 in monthly utility savings that your salesperson promised in a prior e-mail, which it attaches, and it wants to know what you're going to do about it.

You know you've got the law on your side, so you call the university's purchasing agent and point out the pertinent provisions in the P2P Terms and Conditions. He says he's got no idea what you're talking about and asks you if you've read the University Terms and Conditions. You've never heard of the University Terms and Conditions, so he e-mails you a copy. Contrary to your terms and conditions, their form says that the sale is contingent upon conformance with all representations made by the P2P sales department, that all warranty and damage disclaimers are specifically refused, that the university retains the right to sue for consequential damages, and that all disputes are to be determined by way of a lawsuit in their home jurisdiction.

The university files suit in its backyard seeking, among other things, $20,000 a month for the utility savings it was promised. You file for an arbitration in your backyard, seeking full payment plus interest. The university claims the University Terms and Conditions govern the deal. You claim that the P2P Terms and Conditions govern the deal. Both of you say that you never would have made the deal unless the other side agreed to your terms and conditions, and that's what you thought happened. Now what?

Welcome to the battle of the forms.

This sort of thing happens most frequently in transactions involving the sale of goods—in the sense of tangible objects—between businesses, and because of that, the law has crafted a new set of rules in the effort to create some predictability in that specific area. (The traditional mirror image rule continues to govern, for instance, all consumer transactions and all business agreements concerning sales of services, sales of companies, real estate deals, and so on.) The rules are included in a book-length statute that has been adopted throughout the country, known as the Uniform Commercial Code (UCC)—except that not every state has adopted exactly the same version, and different courts in different states have interpreted the same provisions of the UCC in different ways.

The battle of the forms rule is important—too important to pretend that a practical and usable understanding can be conveyed in a few pages. Basically, so long as the parties have agreed on the fundamentals (such as price and quantity), the rules specify a procedure that begins with the effort to find which of the various forms constitutes the offer. That's usually a lot easier said than done, because knowing how the battle of the forms works, each side will style its form as the one, true offer.

Once the offer is identified, its terms will govern, and a binding contract including those terms will be formed—*even if* the responding form contains contrary terms. The key difference from the fundamentals of contract law is this: the responding form will function as an acceptance of the offer even though it is not the mirror image of the offer, and the company that sent the responding form can get stuck with a deal it never really agreed to make.

Not surprisingly (this being the law, after all), there's a hugely important exception: the responding form will *not* be treated as an acceptance of the offer *if* the responding form includes language stating that there's no deal *unless* all of *its* additional terms are agreed to.

It goes downhill from there.

By far, the most important thing to remember about the battle of the forms is this: *you'll never know if you won or lost the battle until it's too late.* You can try to tilt things in your favor with various language and other techniques, but the other side may be playing the game along with you, and when all is said and done, a court or an arbitrator, as the case may be, will be left with a

⇢ **The most important thing to remember about the battle of the forms is this:** *you'll never know if you won or lost the battle until it's too late . . .* **The point of negotiating a contract is to lock in the terms of the deal before it begins, not after it's over. The battle of the forms is no way to do business.**

mishmash of points and counterpoints that defy predictable disentanglement. As the manager of P2P Enterprises, you thought you were locking in contract clauses that were of great importance, such as the warranty disclaimer, the damage disclaimer, and the arbitration provision. The truth is that you won't know whether your clauses are worth a whit until some judge, jury, or arbitrator tells you, months or years after the transaction was completed. The point of negotiating a contract is to lock in the terms of the deal before it begins, not after it's over. The battle of the forms is no way to do business.

The solution is not to fight the battle. If contradictory forms are being exchanged, you need to stop the madness and confront the important issues directly. If the warranty and damage disclaimers are crucial to you, you must either make a stand or decide the risk is worth taking. The same is true with all of the other provisions your form probably addresses—attorneys' fees in the event of nonpayment, where and how disputes are resolved, potential liability for shipping delays, and so on. Either make them part of the agreement, walk away from the deal, or decide you can live without them. This is another situation in which the Attorney Hotline arrangement can prove invaluable.

Look at it this way. Let's suppose you want to buy some raw materials. You go to a lawyer for advice, you tell him what terms you need in the deal with the seller, and you ask him to prepare the documents. He tells you that he'll try, but he can't guarantee that the terms you need will actually end up in the agreement. You can give it a try, he says—pay your money, take your chances, and *maybe* you'll end up with the deal you want. If the raw materials you buy end up being defective, you might be able to collect the damages you suffer from the seller. Maybe not. If there's a dispute, you might be able to litigate in your home court instead of theirs, thousands of miles away. Maybe not. You might have the right to withhold payment until the dust settles without incurring extra charges and attorneys' fees obligations. Maybe not.

If that's acceptable, good luck. If that's not acceptable, don't fight the battle of the forms.

THE GOAL OF A WELL-MANAGED business is not the elimination of *all* potential problems. No one can foresee everything that might surface—and the fruitless quest to do so can become a problem in itself. Moreover, the willingness to take risks, and to incur the problems that sometimes flow from those risks, is a part of virtually every successful business. Without risk, without taking a chance, without being willing to try and to fail, growth is rare.

Instead, the goal must be to eliminate, or at least minimize, the *unnecessary* problems—the problems that spring from ignorance, from not doing what could have been easily done. In the legal context, the unnecessary problems are those that flow from the failure to find and use the copious tools the law provides to keep molehills from becoming mountains, and to elude the battles that don't have to be fought. Let your competition fight and stress over old deals while you focus on new deals. Let them play defense while you play offense.

The concept is beyond self-evident. All companies have a finite amount of time, money, energy, and creativity. For what purposes and how well those resources are utilized define the role of management: the less that is devoted to the unnecessary problems of the past, the more that can be devoted to the achievements of the future. And for many companies—more than you might imagine—therein lies the edge, the advantage, the line between success and failure.

# Acknowledgments

Most of what I have tried to synthesize in this book was garnered from my work with the clients of the Powell, Trachtman, Logan, Carrle & Lombardo, P.C., law firm, many of whom I have represented for more than thirty years. My motivation for writing this book was to give back to them some of what they gave to me—their experiences, their ingenuity, and their wisdom. I hope they will consider this a down payment on a much larger debt of gratitude.

Michael Fragnito at Sterling Publishing gave me the opportunity to write this book, and then followed it with ample helpings of encouragement and guidance. Tricia Medved and Barbara Berger, my editors at Sterling, were wise and patient sounding boards as I wrestled with the task of translating and de-mystifying the law's arcane complexities. Many thanks to each of you for your help, your generosity, and your good humor.

# Index